Be Still and Know

A Mother's Story
of Faith, Heartbreak, & Miracles

By Monique Davis

A special thank you to Diane Schleyhahn
for the beautiful artwork on the cover
that brought The Holy Spirit's vision to life.

With Thanks To My Prayer Warriors:
Sherrie
Angie
Debbie
Jan
Don
Jennifer
Judy
Stacie
and Momma

I thank God every time
I remember you.
In all my prayers for all of you,
I always pray with joy because of
your partnership in the gospel
from the first day until now.
--Philippians 1:3-4

Prologue

The Storm Before the Calm

I don't really remember if we were quiet or loud as we drove down the country road that night. I do remember it was a cold night, and the stars seemed brighter than normal. As my mother rounded a corner and turned into our driveway, which seemed like a half mile long, I saw his truck. Rocks popped and crackled in the crisp December air as we edged closer to our house. My excitement was growing because he had told me he would be gone before I got home. But in the starlit night, I could plainly see that my dad was still there.

I don't remember when tension began to fill the car. My self-focused seven-year-old brain was celebrating that he wasn't gone. I don't even remember getting out of the car, but I do remember walking into the house and quickly scanning the living room before walking into the kitchen and finding my father, shotgun across his lap, cleaning rag in hand, and an oil can sitting on the kitchen table; nothing unusual about this. Dad hunted a lot. In fact, in those days, if we ate any meat at all, it came from his experienced and successful ability to hunt. Rabbit, quail, squirrel, deer, geese, ducks, Dad was the victor.

I don't remember how much time passed before I knew they were fighting. In fact, after all these years, I still don't really recall the fight, just flashes of images or clips of the movie of that night remain in my head. The freezer door open to expose several glasses full of ice (prepared for a soon to come holiday dinner), a hole on the kitchen wall where the telephone was supposed to be, my uncle's back as he sat on the living room couch pretending to watch TV, and my mother pacing with my 18-day-old brother in her arms.

The next thing I remember was all the glass. There was glass scattered like square, sharp, different sized marbles that completely covered the floor as I attempted to tip-toe through the contents of what had been in the freezer. Although, I don't remember hearing him throw the glasses at Mother, but that night, there had to have been no escaping the sound.

In the middle of this sharp sea, sat my dad in a medium blue slimmed down recliner-style chair with light brown wooden arms. His head was in his hands, fingers laced through his hair. He was slumped over. I wiggled my way onto his lap, forcing him to sit up a bit. I tried to kiss him goodnight, missing my target but successfully connecting with his scruffy cheek, as he quickly turned his head and the familiar scent of whiskey overwhelmed me.

"Good Night, Daddy."

His response was silence.

I don't know how I fell asleep so quickly, other than that the leagues of angels watching over my family that night made sure of it. My 12-year-old sister was not so lucky, as the sounds of this night haunt her still today. I have no idea how much time passed, how much arguing occurred, or how many threats were hurled before my 21-year-old uncle decided to bolt from the couch to summon the police.

The next thing I knew, my uncle was lifting me from deep sleep, holding my head tightly to his chest and placing me in the back of a car next to my 12-year-old sister. I had no idea what was going on, but the air was heavy with something. Fear?

We drove to my grandparents' home. It felt like it was 2 a.m., 3 a.m.? I kept asking, "Where is my mother?" No one would really say anything. I was told to keep quiet and get into the bed my grandmother had made up for me. I lay there in the dark, but the dim kitchen light told me the adults were up talking.

I awoke with a start. Silence filled the house, and as I crept to the back room, across the wooden floors, I was silent. When I pushed back the door, the outline of a body that was my mother's was underneath the chenille quilt. She turned to me, lifted the covers, and motioned for me to slide into the bed next to her. No words, just silence. I obeyed, the fear engulfing me, threatening to squeeze me to extinction. My mother cried softly as I watched her beautiful face lined with a grief, I would later understand, her brown eyes filled to overflowing with anguish.

"Where is my daddy?" I asked in the deafening silence.

"Where do you think he is?" Her voice was in complete controlled-contrast to her face. There was a calm that didn't fit. (I felt her swallow and take a breath.)

"Is he in jail?"

"Monique, your daddy's dead."

As the years passed, I would learn bits and pieces of what happened on that December 21st. I would learn that a few miles from our home, my great-grandmother, Gladys Bowen, was awakened from her sleep with an overwhelming need to pray. As she climbed out of bed and onto her knees, she didn't know why, but she began to pray for the safety of my family. She prayed and prayed, not knowing what was happening in our home, but she was consumed by the need to pray for our protection.

After I went to sleep that dreadful night, my mother had managed to put to bed my 15-month-old sister and 18-day-old brother in the midst of my father's drunken, violent rage. All of my mother's four children were in their beds and asleep, or so she thought, as she walked up the main hallway of our home. The fear must have been overwhelming and heavy as she went to face her husband in the midst of his uncontrolled emotions.

She expected to find him in the kitchen, where he had last been. However, where she found my father would be the final place he would ever take a breath or speak a word. This place was my bedroom.

As I lay sleeping, my father entered my bedroom, gun in hand, and sat on the side of my bed.

Mother was silent when her body filled my bedroom doorway, but he knew she was there. He sat stroking my hair with his gun across his lap.

"I'm taking her with me."

She reacted without thought, her maternal instinct completely taking over. She pushed my dad out of the way and scooped me up from my bed and ran down the hallway, not sure if he was pursuing her. After depositing me into her bed, she slowly crept back towards my room.

The first shot went through my bedroom ceiling.

"Good-bye, Pam."

The second shot was followed by the sound of a body falling to the floor.

She stood there for a moment, not sure if he was playing cat and mouse, luring her into a trap, and then the doorbell rang. My mother ran for the door and found a female police officer standing there.

Once it was verified that my father was gone, they began questioning my mother, at first implying she may have been the cause of my father's death, but they quickly realized the truth of that night.

On Christmas Eve of 1977, I stood looking at my father in a casket, praying that God would make him blink, move, wake up, but it never happened. I would spend the next several years trying to understand why this horrible night happened, asking where God was in the midst of this tragedy. Until one day, I was able to be thankful for the blessings and the protection that were given to my family that night.

I slept through my father coming into my room; I can only imagine what may have happened if I hadn't. My uncle was able to alert the police. My sisters, brother, and mother were all alive, and my mother had saved my life.

My ears had heard of you,

but now my eyes have seen you.

--Job 42:5

Chapter One

As someone who has lived through more than most could bear, I have found great comfort in knowing that God is in control. In the unexplainable, excruciatingly painful experiences that make no sense to me, I have clung to this truth. God has a perfect plan. He is creating something MUCH larger than I. I am a thread, and HE is creating a beautiful tapestry. I can only see the backside of the tapestry, and it is an ugly mess. But in the end, when God turns it over, it will be an artistic masterpiece.

I have clung to the truth that I do NOT need to understand. I stopped asking why because most of the time there are no answers. Just knowing that the Bible says we cannot know God's ways gives me so much comfort. It assures me that I'm actually not supposed to get it.

"For my thoughts are not your thoughts, neither are your ways my ways, declares the LORD. As the heavens are higher than the earth, so are my ways higher than your ways and my thoughts than your thoughts." --Isaiah 55:8-9

15

November 2010

I am bored and lonely in my hotel room. I have been in San Francisco for several days at a public speaking conference. I know no one, but that doesn't stop me from seeing all that the city has to offer. I ride a trolley, I shop in Chinatown, I walk down by the wharf, and I visit Alcatraz. But traveling alone is definitely not my thing. Although the hotel where I am staying is nice, I miss my family and wish I were at home.

I am lying on the fluffy bed, surrounded by too many pillows, eating noodles I had just picked up from a fun little place I had discovered in Chinatown, when my phone rings. The screen tells me it is Alex.

"Mom, I need you to pray for Joe Brady. Someone said he tried to commit suicide tonight," Alex says, clearly concerned.

"What? What are you talking about? How do you know this?" I say, deciding in that moment to not give Alex the "know your source" talk.

"Someone said something on Facebook."

"Of course, I will pray for him."
Memories flash through my mind of December 1977. The amount of guilt that survivors of suicide are left with is often overwhelming, and knowing how tender and compassionate my 15-

year-old son is, I know that he could easily fall prey to this dark truth.

"Alex, I want you to know something that has taken me many years to learn. When someone commits suicide, there is NOTHING you could have done, should have done, or shouldn't have done that would change the outcome. If someone really wants to take his or her own life, no one changes that."

He listens, but is clearly distracted by his thoughts. I tell him that I love him and that I'll be home Sunday, before we end the phone call.

I finish up the noodles and begin my nighttime routine. I clean and moisturize my face, floss and brush my teeth, and change into a pair of loose-fitting shorts and a t-shirt before flopping back on the bed into the numerous pillows. The bookmark that should be holding my place has fallen out, and it takes me several minutes to find it in the mounds of fluff surrounding me. It takes me a few more minutes to discover exactly where I stopped reading, but once I find it, I am immediately pulled back into the story. I have been reading for less than an hour when the ding of my text notification sounds. I pick up my phone and read the message.

Heart racing, I dial Alex's number. He answers after one ring.

"He's dead Mom," Alex cries.

"How do you KNOW this?"

" I KNOW it. It is all over Facebook and Tom said so," he says even more emotionally.

"Oh, Alex. Honey, I'm so so sorry." My heart is hurting for him; a panic is welling up inside of me. "Are you alone?"

"Yes. Dad is home, but I'm in my room."

"Did you tell Dad?"

"No. I just found out," he is sobbing now.

"Sweetheart, I'm coming home. I'll get a flight and be home as soon as I can."

I need to be home as quickly as possible. I am throwing my clothes into my suitcase as I dial Jeff and fill him in on what is happening. But I quickly discover that I will have to wait to leave until tomorrow in the late morning. I fall to my knees and cry out.

"Abba, Father, surround Alex right now; comfort him in this time of loss. Father, be present with Joe's family right now. Please send a peace that will hold them together. Father, how do you lose a child and survive or even want to survive? Oh, Father, please comfort his family."

18

Chapter Two

The church is packed with more sobbing teenagers and parents than I can count. The experience is gut-wrenching. Watching Joe's parents greet each individual who has come to give condolences is almost more than I can bear. Alex sits with his friends. I am seated not far from him; I'm there for whenever he needs me. I'm not exactly sure how all this works; how do you help your 15-year-old son deal with the grief that comes from losing a friend to suicide?

Alex is at Tom's, our youth pastor's, house constantly in the first few days after Joe's death. I don't like Alex being gone so much, but I know that there are many kids from the youth group who are also staying at Tom's house, so I let Alex too. This seems to be how the kids are dealing with this tragic loss, by being together, but all I want to do is wrap Alex up in my arms and hold him and tell him that it will be OK.

I have been home from San Francisco for a week before Alex and I finally have a chance to sit down and really talk.

"On Sunday night, I was at youth-group, and was getting a ride home from Tom. He knew something was going on with Joe. As we drove home, we passed an ambulance, and I felt this sick feeling; I just knew Joe was in there. Tom drove straight to Joe's house, parked the car, and told me not to get out. Then he went inside. There were police cars all over the place, and Joe's parents' van was pulled into the font yard."

"When Tom came back out, I knew it was bad, but he said nothing. As he dropped me off at home, he said he was heading to the hospital. At that point, he didn't know if Joe was alive or dead, but he knew that Joe was on his way to the hospital and that he had tried to hang himself. I should have been there, Mom. Joe put a message on Facebook. We were at church. No one saw it. If I had been with him…" Alex says, overtaken by tears and unable to finish his sentence.

"Alex honey, remember, there is nothing you could have done. If he really wanted to hurt himself, there is no one who could have stopped it," I say wrapping him in my arms as we both cried. "I'm so so sorry. I know how this hurts. I wish I could just wipe this hurt away."

"Mom, I need you to know that you are going to start hearing about me hanging out with some people that you wouldn't approve of. They need me, Mom. Joe needed me, but I wasn't there. That isn't going to happen again."

"What do you mean, Alex?"

"Well, they do things you won't approve of."

"Like?"

"Drink, drugs, lots of stuff."

"Alex, this is what you want to stay away from," I say, keeping in mind the natural desire to be independent and rebellious that comes along with being 15.

"Mom, even if you tell me I can't hang out with them, I'm going to do it anyway. They need to know Jesus. I need to save them."

I am impressed with his conviction, but a little taken aback at his defiance. He has always been such a compliant kid; never a problem, always such an obedient boy. I know he is a good kid, and I tell myself that this is just the grief talking. I say a silent prayer as I respond to him.

"I really admire your desire to be a good influence and to save your friends, but you need to know that you aren't strong enough to withstand the temptations that can come by hanging out with people like that. It really scares me. Evil can easily overtake us when we aren't in the places we are supposed to be."

21

"I'll be OK, Mom. But they need me, and I'm going to be there."

Time passes and Alex is still spending a lot of time away from home. The kids aren't staying at the youth pastor's house anymore, instead, they are at the Brady's. Alex is becoming more and more distant and irritable. This is completely new territory for me. Alex has always been so sweet; we have always been so close. I'm convinced that this is grief, but I don't really know how to help him. I try to give him his space, but I also try to talk when the occasion allows. He is less and less willing to tell me anything, and I am beginning to get concerned.

Then I receive a phone call from a concerned parent telling me that he had just caught his own son smoking pot and wanted to let me know that Alex is smoking it too. My head begins to spin. Alex? Alex Davis? My Alex? Smoking pot?

I wait until I knew what I wanted to say before approaching Alex. I don't know what I expected, but his answer to my question was not it.

"I'm smoking pot to keep from killing myself," he sobbed, falling into my arms.

My heart immediately began to race; I could feel it pulsing in my temples. Kill yourself? I couldn't lose Alex. Suicide? How had I missed this depression? Guilt encompassed me.

We talk for a long time. Just like old times, but tonight the conversation wasn't about school, or church, or dreams; tonight, it was about fighting to not die. I slept in his room that night, afraid to leave him alone, afraid of what may happen.

I call the doctor first thing in the morning. I let Alex sleep in and called him in sick for school. After the doctor's appointment, Alex begins taking antidepressants. I felt hopeful, but a new fear was building inside me.

Chapter Three

On the Friday before my spring break, I realize that Alex has forgotten to grab his lunch before he headed to the bus stop. I grab it, and run out the front door, hoping to catch him before the bus gets there. But as I round the corner of the house, I catch a glimpse of Alex standing at the side of our house. He quickly turns away and tries to hide something. I realize he is smoking something, and I can't believe my eyes. He tries to stuff something into his pocket, and as I get closer, the aroma of marijuana fills the air. I make him empty his pockets into my hands. I am furious but in shock. I tell him to get into the house because we need to talk. He says he is going to be late for school, and instead he runs for the bus. It is in this moment that I realize we have a much bigger problem on our hands.

The first phone call I make is to Alex's doctor's office. I'm in completely unfamiliar territory; I don't know what to do, but I know I have to do something. As I wait for the nurse to return the message I have left, I am scurrying around to get out the door, so that I will get to work on time. Once in the car, I begin to pray for God to give me wisdom to know how to deal with what is happening to Alex and the strength to do it.

The nurse tells me that our doctor wants Jeff and me to take Alex to Lincoln Prairie Behavioral Center to have him evaluated. She tells us that this facility is for kids, and they deal with emotional illnesses and drug use. My heart is beating as it never has before, while a cloud of impending doom begins to surround it. Could this really be me discussing taking Alex to a facility like this?

Jeff and I decide we will take Alex after we eat dinner that night. I make spaghetti, salad, and bread. I know it is something Alex likes, and my maternal instinct says to give him a good meal, to make sure he is full, before we begin this extremely terrifying task.

The dinner table is pretty silent. Alex must be waiting for his dad and me to discuss what happened that morning, but his little brother is at the dinner table, so Alex must feel somewhat protected by this fact. When dinner is over, I begin to clean up the kitchen.

"Go get some shoes on," Jeff says in Alex's direction.

"Are we going somewhere?" Alex asks his dad.

"Just get your shoes on," Jeff replies.

My heart is pounding so hard in my chest now; I swear Alex must be able to see it. I become very quiet, a survival skill I have honed since I was a child. I, too, put on my shoes, and we all climb into the car. Our drive is silent. I'm sure Alex's mind must have been racing as he tried to figure out what was happening. But there is no hiding our location when we pull up to the facility.

"Are you serious?" Alex blurts out.

"Just get out of the car with your mom," Jeff demands.

The attendant at the front desk knew that we were coming. Dr. Sandercock's office had called to arrange the evaluation. As we sit in a room with an intake specialist, she begins to ask Alex questions.

Alex is forthcoming with his feelings of depression, thoughts of suicide, and drug use. He talks about losing his friend to suicide. Tears slip down my cheeks as he talks. It is as if his sadness is seeping into my soul.

When the decision to admit him comes, I can feel a panic curl around me.

"I don't want to stay here," Alex's eyes, wide with panic, lock on mine.

"You need help, Buddy," is all I can say and still manage to hold back my desire to fall on the floor and sob.

Paperwork to admit Alex is put in front of Jeff and me. As the contents of what we are being asked to sign is explained, I begin to wonder if there isn't some hidden clause in the paperwork that allows this facility to take Alex away from us permanently. I shake away this irrational fear and sign my name.

The attendant takes Alex's shoes, belt, and all his personal belongings. They make him change into clothing they provide. My mind is racing. Is this the right decision? Can't I just take him home? What if he does actually try to hurt himself, and I'm not there to stop it? I could never forgive myself. I am thankful that Jeff is there because his strength is what enables me to put one foot in front of the other as we follow Alex and the attendant through a long hallway to locked doors and onto a locked elevator.

When we reach the floor where Alex will be, I notice how quiet it is. Jeff and I are escorted to a room where someone explains the treatment process, and Alex is taken in a different direction. He doesn't even look at me as he is led away.

I sit in the room listening to the nurse discuss what the schedule will be like for Alex while he is in the program. I try to listen well and ask questions, but my heart feels as though someone has trampled it, and my brain cannot overcome the pain. Jeff and I are led to the same elevator that brought us to this floor. We stand with the nurse, her key in the wall, summoning the car to the correct floor. I am openly crying now. The nurse assures me that Alex will be well taken care of, that I can call and speak to a nurse and check in on him at any time, and that I can visit. She hands me a copy of the paperwork we signed, along with an informational brochure.

When the elevator doors close, I cannot hold it together any longer, and I begin to sob uncontrollably and almost fall to the floor as Jeff catches me. It is a cry of fear but mostly a cry of loss. A broken heartedness encompasses me, and I am gasping for air as I walk to our SUV and climb into my seat. It is a good thing Jeff is there to drive.

Alex spends three weeks at this facility. We visit at every available opportunity. He willingly attends the individual and group counseling sessions, and when the time to discharge him comes, we are very hopeful that he is now moving in the correct direction. Unfortunately, this is a short-lived hope.

Chapter Four

Alex tries to get back into the groove of going to school. He appears to be working to catch up on the schoolwork he missed while at Lincoln Prairie, but it doesn't take long for him to begin to push the boundaries. He breaks curfew, he talks back, he leaves when he is told he cannot, and we notice his grades are slipping. Jeff and I impose new parameters and new consequences to Alex's freedom, but it doesn't seem to help much.

The first time I knew that he had sneaked out, it was storming. The thunder reverberated throughout the walls of the house and the rattling of the glass in the windows made it so I could not sleep. It had been a habit of mine to check on my boys while they slept since they were born. I don't know how many times I would creep into their rooms just to watch their chests rise and fall or hear them softly exhale.

Lightning lit up the house as I walked down to the basement where Alex's room was. As I reached for his door handle, I was shocked to find it locked. I quickly found the key to open his door and to my horror found Alex's bed empty.

My mind was racing. Thunder could be felt reverberating throughout the walls with a force that made my knees weak. The storm was so severe. Where could he be? I dialed his number, and it went to voicemail. I hung up and dialed again....voicemail. I text him.

WHERE ARE YOU????

No response and the message does not show "Read." My heart pounding, I pace back and forth trying to clear my mind so that I can think.

It was at this point that I realized the new technology of cell phones meant that I had no phone numbers for any of his friends' parents. There was a time when I had all of the home numbers of all of his friends, but now that his friends carried phones themselves, that practice of mine had gone by the wayside. I told myself that I must remember to start making a new list. Then I remembered that I had a school directory, so at 2 a.m. I began making phone calls to find my boy.

After several calls, I find one friend who thinks he knows where Alex might be. His mother offers Jeff and me the opportunity to pick up her son, so that he can show us where Alex is. So, at almost 3 a.m., Jeff and I pick up Wayne, and we drive to a not so nice part of town to a tall white building. In the back of this building, we find Alex's parked car. Wayne tells us that Troy lives here, and Alex visits him often.

Jeff and I knock on the front door for some time, as Wayne waits in our SUV, hoping not to be discovered as the informant, but no one answers. We then go to a side door and knock on the glass, no answer. We return to the front door. No answer. I dial Alex's number again. Voicemail.

I can hear someone behind the door and all of a sudden it opens. Troy is standing there trying to look as innocent as possible.

"Where is Alex?" Jeff barks.

"I don't know, sir. He isn't here," Troy answers a little too quickly, a little too politely.

"We know he is here. His car is parked right behind your place."

"His car is here? I don't know why his car would be here, but he isn't," Troy says as he closes the door.

At this point, we are in shock. Jeff wants to kick the door down, but we call 911 instead. Within about 15 minutes, a police officer rolls up, and we quickly explain the situation. The officer talks to us a bit about the kind of neighborhood we are in and tells us it is a good thing that we decided to call. He also says that the Springfield Police Department is no stranger to this address.

This time, when the officer knocks, Alex answers the door.

"What is your name?" The officer questions.

"That's our son," I blurt out.

"I'm Alexander Davis," Alex replies.

"I need you to come out of there and go home with your parents," the officer says.

Troy is nowhere to be seen or heard. Alex comes out closing the front door behind him. The officer reads Alex the riot act for sneaking out, causing us worry, and for being at this particular house. Alex listens politely to the officer, but I can see he is holding back his anger like a racehorse being held back at the starting gate. When the officer finishes his attempt at curtailing Alex's ever doing this again, Jeff and I lock eyes and remember that Wayne is hiding in the SUV, and we do not want to betray his trust in us.

"You take the SUV and go on home. I'll drive Alex and his car home," Jeff says.

As I drive Wayne home, he and I talk. We talk about his past and the fact that he is trying to get his act together after getting kicked out of school the year before. He tells me that he is worried about Alex hanging out with Troy and that Alex has been hanging out with him a lot. A small voice in my head whispers something to me about Wayne being jealous of Troy, but I push it away and assure myself that Wayne is really a good kid who just made a bad choice and now he is really trying to redeem himself. As I drop him off at his house, I again thank him for helping us find Alex tonight, and I promise that neither Alex's dad nor I will say anything about his help.

Chapter Five

There were many sleepless nights in the beginning, once we knew things weren't right. I found myself waking up all hours of the night and walking the stairs down to the first floor through the dining room and kitchen, down the basement steps, through the darkened area to Alex's closed and lock door. Finding the key that I used to trip the lock, I would tremble at what I would find. Would he be breathing? Would he be hanging from the ceiling? Or would he be gone? I would feel relief if my hand touched him safely sleeping in his bed. I would back out of the room quietly, not wanting to disturb him. I would feel panic if I quietly patted, then frantically slapped his empty mattress. Gone, again! Out his window. It's 3 a.m.

I lost track of how many times I tried to hunt him down. Some nights I was victorious; some nights I had no clue where to even begin to look. Sometimes I knew where he was, but he would flat out refuse to come home. How do you get someone with the body of a linebacker to do anything he doesn't want to do? He wasn't allowed to use the car, and we weren't giving him money. I was not prepared to tell him he couldn't live in our home anymore. I always wanted him to know where he belonged and that he was always welcome there. There were many times when I knew Jeff wanted to kick him out and say he couldn't come back, but Jeff knew I was vehemently against this, and thankfully he never pushed me.

The amount of time Alex was gone began to extend. He was sometimes missing for days, sometimes weeks. He stopped going to school. I would call the school sometimes just to see if he was there.

Another night of Alex not coming home.

"Where's Alex?" Drew, our younger son, asks.

"I don't know," I say as I try to swallow the lump in my throat and breathe through the hole in my heart.

"Oh," is his only reply.

It's October 2011, and Alex has been missing for days. Or maybe I should say hasn't come home for days. He shows me some mercy and sends me one text each day.

```
I'm alive.
I love you.
Don't worry.
```

It has been such a confusing dichotomy. After all, as Alex tells me, he isn't trying to hurt me. He just wants to do what he wants, when he wants, but he cannot fathom why I am not OK with that. He does not want to respect my rules or what I say, but somehow he wants to ease my fear through all this. "God, let him know that I love him, that I will never stop loving him."

His entire future, everything I have dreamed for him, planned for him, and hoped for him was getting dimmer with each passing day. The pain I felt was visceral. I could feel a pressure in my chest as if someone were pushing down trying to stop my lungs from taking in air. Yes, it was a physical, undeniable pain. I cried so often it was the norm.

During this time, I was a traveling teacher. I traveled to three schools every day. I would pray and sing and sob my way to one school, pull myself together, go teach, get back into my car, and sob and pray and plead with God to tell me what to do, how to save my baby from the path he was treading. I would get to another school, pull myself back together, teach, and get back into my car, and the process would start all over again. Every day for four months this was my pattern.

"Please, God, save my baby."

The first time I heard God speak, it wasn't as if I actually heard a voice. It was instead a REALLY LOUD thought. I was in pieces emotionally. I was crying out to the Lord with every molecule in my human body.

"God, please save my baby. Save my baby. God, save my baby. Save my baby."

Then I heard it.

"I already have."

It took me by surprise, the truth in this moment. God, the God of the universe, was reminding me of His promise. "Anyone who calls out my name, I will send thousands of angels to save you," an amazing gift that I shouldn't forget.

I knew that Alex was saved, and even though he surely wasn't living that way now. In fact, he was denying he believed at all, but I knew that salvation could not be taken away. God had already saved Alex from himself, from sin, from eternal death.

This was a message, sent directly from God that was MEANT FOR ME. It was meant as an encouragement, to remind me that God was listening to me, and that He was way ahead of me.

My prayer then changed to one of gratitude.

"Thank you, God for saving him and for ensuring us that salvation does not have an expiration date."

God was there beside me, just as He had promised He would be. I knew that even though I couldn't be with Alex, even though I couldn't save him from his choices, God could. Not only could He, but He had ALREADY done it!

"The LORD your God is with you, He is mighty to save. He will take great delight in you; he will quiet you with His love. He will rejoice over you with singing."

--Zephaniah 3:17

My dependence on God was growing. I poured my fear and pain out to Him constantly; it was my time to cry and to be held.

"Oh, God! I love this boy. I'm so scared of what might happen to him. Where is he sleeping? What is he eating? Is he taking his medicine? What kind of people is he being exposed to? I bet the place is dirty. Why would he stay in such a place? He has never lived in an unsafe or unclean home before. What is drawing him there now?"

Pressure in the middle of my chest was threatening to extinguish me; it worsened or lessened, but never seemed to be gone during these days. "Just breathe," I heard God whisper.

Chapter Six

"Alex why are you doing this? Why do you keep running?" I asked one day when he slipped in the door to retrieve some clean clothes and sneak in a shower.

"I want you to just leave me alone. Stop coming to where I am. Stop trying to make me come home," he yelled through the door.

I waited patiently until his door opened. I looked him straight in the eye.

"I will NEVER stop loving you. There is nothing you could do that would EVER make me stop loving you. I will continue to hunt you down and drag you back until my last dying breath."

"I just need you to stop loving me," he says angrily.

"Sorry, not a chance. I will never stop," I say with all the conviction I have left.

"Well, you need to," he says over his shoulder as he walks out the front door and gets into a waiting car. I stand in the doorway, tears streaming down my face, hoping he will look my way, just a glance in my direction is all I need, but Alex's head is turned away as the car disappears.

I spend every available moment searching for help for Alex. It is clear that his drug use is increasing and his life is out of control. I begin to hear rumors that he is dealing, but this too is something over which I have no control.

I have told God over and over that I would do whatever He wanted me to do. I just needed Him to TELL ME! I begged God to lead me to what he wanted me to do. I would ask over and over for God to make what I'm supposed to do as clear as a burning bush, so that there was no chance I could miss His direction.

"God, just please tell me."

I knew God was hearing me, but as Alex fell deeper into his pit, nothing was clear. I made phone calls to every agency I could think of: drug rehab facilities, boys' homes, churches, Focus on the Family, doctors, the police, the truancy officer, the school, anyone who worked with troubled teens. I called locally. I called places within the State of Illinois and across the entire country. Somebody please help me save my baby, I begged. Over and over again I was told it was not the right fit for Alex for one reason or another.

"Has your son been in trouble with the law?"

"No! I'm trying to get him help before that happens!"

"Well, ma'am, there isn't much we can do until a judge mandates that he come to our facility. We cannot force him to stay if he doesn't want to stay, unless he is ordered to do so. Illinois is a Child Right State, which means no one, including minors, can be forced into rehab."

"Are you kidding me? What are we supposed to do? How are we supposed to help him?"

"I know it is frustrating, and there needs to be more options for parents, but I'm sorry."

I search the web for weeks. There are many places that take "troubled boys," but what was a good place, which one could I trust? And how on earth can we afford it? Fees of $5,000, $10,000 a month for up to 12 months? What price do you put on your son's life? Do you give everything up for him? What if you aren't sure it will work? What then?

"Tell me what to do, God! Show me, God! I need it to be clear, so that I cannot miss it! Tell me, God, what to do! Please make it clear!"

I expand my search to all over the country and begin to seriously consider a program out of state. I do find a place that sounds like it may work, but it is in the Northwest, and my fear of Alex feeling abandoned causes me to rule it out.

God has always spoken to me through an unexplainable peace, a feeling that makes my soul calm even when everything around me is far from it. I knew that He would again. I just had to wait.

"Your timing is perfect God. Help me to believe that. Help me to make it through today, just today God. Let Alex call me. Let him sleep in his bed tonight. Let me hold him for a moment and tell him I love him."

One day as I am on the phone telling our story once again, begging for help, I received the same response I have received several times. "Not the right program because he hasn't been arrested." I began to cry as the woman clearly feels helpless.

"I'm so sorry. I wish I had an answer. Because Illinois is a "Child Right" state, children cannot be forced into a facility unless it is court mandated. There needs to be more options for parents," she says.

"I'm trying so hard to get him help before he gets into serious trouble. I have looked everywhere, but I can find nothing," I say, trying to not completely lose it on the phone.

Just as I am about to hang up, the woman says, "You know, I heard about this place outside of Bloomington. Uhhh, something ranch. I'm not sure what it is called. Maybe, Salem Ranch? I'm sure you can find it on the web. There cannot be too many places outside of Bloomington. I don't know anything about their program, but you might want to look into it."

"OK, thank you," I say. I can feel something deep down telling me this is the place even before I begin to search on the Internet.

Within a few minutes of searching, I find it: Salem Youth Ranch. It is a Christian horse farm in the middle of nowhere. They accept boys only. I make a phone call and talk to someone at the ranch for a while. This program sounds as though it may be a good option for Alex, and a bud of hope is growing. But the program is expensive, $5,000 a month. How on earth could we afford that?

I put those reservations aside as I call Jeff and tell him what I have found. The excitement in my own voice catches me off guard as I realize exactly what I am suggesting. That we again send our son away, but this time it would be much further away and for a much longer time, and worst of all, Alex would not go willingly. We decided to tour the ranch, and I made the arrangements.

Chapter Seven

My whole life I have tried to be in control. I am a careful planner, a list maker, a doer. I set goals and dates by which to meet them, and I rarely miss. My entire life I have tried to make the life I wanted and needed. It wasn't until this experience with Alex that I completely relinquished control. And it was the scariest most faith dependent step I have ever taken in my life.

God took me to a place where the chaos of our situation was unquestionable, and my inability to calm the storm was painfully apparent. I fought long and hard to fix it all, to find the answers for our issues, but as our world spun further and further out of control, God was teaching me to trust Him. To trust even though I could not see; He knew exactly what was happening. He would be the one to stop the spinning, when and only when He knew the time was right, when the lessons that we were supposed to learn from all of this were learned, when God knew we were ready to truly surrender to His will.

I had told Alex repetitively that I would NEVER stop loving him. That there was NOTHING he could EVER do that would change this. He could try to push me away, but I wasn't going anywhere. I was always going to accept him back, as many times as it took. As painful as it was to watch him hurt himself, as clear as it was for me to see what he needed to do to stop his pain, I would wait. I would chase him down and drag him back over and over and over again. He could not outrun my love. Even when it hurt, when the pain threatened to swallow me, even when I mourned for him, I never once thought about giving up or leaving or pushing him away. I would have died for Alex if it had been a necessary choice. I would suffer. I would do whatever God told me to do. I just needed God to lead me to what He wanted me to do.

The second time I heard God's voice, it was Monday morning. I was in my car, between schools, and I was crying out to my Abba.

"I will never stop loving this boy. I will never stop loving him! I will NEVER STOP LOVING HIM! NEVER STOP LOVING HIM! Oh, God! Let him know I will never stop loving him. I will never stop loving him! Please, God!"

Then I heard that voice in my head again. It was strong and clear and unmistakable.

"Now you get it. The way you feel for this boy, your son, is how I feel for you. My love for you is immeasurable. My love for Alex is immeasurable. As much as you love him, it does not even rival my love for him. How much more do I want him to come home? I have plans for him. Let me have him. You can trust me with him."

The truth in this hit me, and all of a sudden, it made complete sense. God loves me, and he loves Alex. All of my hopes and plans and thoughts for Alex's life, his future, pale to what God has in store. I began to think about how I would die for my children without question, without hesitation. I would save them if that would ever present itself.

As soon as this thought crossed my mind, another revelation exploded in my head: Christ had already done that! He HAD died for me already! He was presented with the option and without hesitation, He chose to die to save me.

"Oh, God! Forgive me. Forgive me for things I have done. For times I have run from you, for times I have dishonored you, for times I have disobeyed you, for times I have not listened to you. I want to do your will, God. I want to trust you, to follow your will for my life and for the lives of my boys," I cry, tears streaming down my face.

An image flashes through my mind. I am carrying Alex in my arms. His much larger frame spills over mine. I am walking up steps to a throne. I see the feet of Jesus, sandaled, bearing scars, and as I lay Alex at His feet, I back away with my head bowed, my arms raised, with praise, with humility, with reverence, and in surrender.

"He is totally yours, God. Take him. You are in control. I can do nothing. I am powerless. But you, you are the God of everything. You can move mountains. You can take this mess and make it into a masterpiece. You can make Alex whole. He is yours God. Take him and help me to believe, help me to know that you are GOD."

"I am still confident of this: I will see the goodness of the LORD in the land of the living. Wait for the LORD; be strong, and take heart and wait for the LORD."

--Psalm 27:13-14

Chapter Eight

It is one of those fall days when the sun is nowhere to be found, and in its place is a blanket of lonely grey clouds. The air is very crisp, and the wind is making it feel even colder. Jeff and I have decided to tour Salem Youth Ranch, which is a little over an hour drive from our home. As we drive down country roads flanked by already harvested cornfields, I am surrounded by an unexplainable calm. The thought of sending Alex away makes me physically sick to my stomach, but something deep inside tells me that this may be the answer for which I have been so desperately praying.

When we finally pull the car into a parking area, which is just in front of a main building, I struggle to keep away the negative thoughts that are starting to invade. I'm not sure if it is my sad heart or the grey clouds that make the building seem so gloomy. I am silently praying for God to help Jeff and me to be on the same page, so that the decision will not have to be mine, and so that the direction in which we are to go will be obvious.

We are greeted by a staff member. She talks with us, explaining the program, while we sit in a small office. She calls for someone to show us around the grounds. There are several horses on the ranch, and the boys are given more responsibilities for the horses as they progress through the program. There is a large open area in a barn where the horses can be ridden and trained on days when they cannot be taken outside. There are stalls to be mucked, horses to be fed and watered, large vegetable gardens to be tended, and other jobs as necessary to keep a ranch successfully running.

The ranch also has a school that allows the boys, most of whom are behind in their credits, to catch up and even graduate from high school if they complete the requirements from the State of Illinois. There are also various opportunities to learn new skills, like woodworking, constructing buildings, and just about anything that goes along with rearing horses. The program is built to teach the boys how to work hard and follow rules. Boys in the program earn privileges as they follow the rules and complete assigned tasks. The ranch has about 100 boys in the program, and all of them have had serious issues with behavior like drug use, stealing, or fighting. The ranch's program also requires the boys to participate in both group and individual therapy.

After our tour, Jeff and I return to the same little office in the main building. I ask all kinds of questions. Among other things, I find out that the length of the program varies depending on each individual, but most residents stay 6-12 months on average. At $5,000 a month, my head is spinning as to how we will afford it. It is then that the woman we are speaking to tells us that they can reduce the fee depending on our income. This help is due to the individuals who have chosen to financially support the program, so that anyone who needs it can attend. We find out that our rate will be $3,000 a month. This is a healthy reduction, but still a hefty price. I quickly do the simple math in my head. If Alex stays for a year, we will be looking at $36,000.

I am trying not to worry. After all, if God wants Alex to go to this program, He will provide the way. I push away the desire to figure out every single detail and decide, instead, to ask God to help me to surrender to His will. I am also concentrating on not tipping my hand to Jeff. I want him to come to his own opinion about this program. I do not want to influence his initial thoughts by telling him mine. I want God to speak to me by letting Jeff and me be on the same page.

I can remember telling myself to be silent as Jeff and I got into our SUV to drive home. I wanted to hear everything Jeff was thinking, but after over 20 years of marriage, I have learned that he needs more time to process than I do, and I really did want to know what he was thinking without my opinion biasing his. Only music filled the car as we drove. I tried to concentrate on the cloud formation in the sky as I sang to myself and prayed.

"What do you think about it?" I ask Jeff after some time had passed.

"I think it has Alex written all over it," he answered without hesitation.

"Me too," I said as tears begin to fill my eyes.

"How are we going to pay for it?" he questions.

"We can use a credit card. I don't know any other way right now."

I begin to think about Joe's parents. What price would they pay to have their son back? Was there any amount they would not pay? If they had been given an opportunity to save Joe, no matter the cost, would they not have paid it? I would spend any amount to rescue my Alex. I wouldn't care if I were in financial debt for the rest of my life. If it meant saving my son, I would do it.

The decision was made to send Alex to the ranch just after Thanksgiving. In the meantime, I was secretly packing for him to go. Jeff and I were given a list of items Alex would need, and so I purchased clothing, shoes, winter-gear, toiletries, and bedding. I tried not to take much from his closet and drawers, so that he wouldn't be curious about things disappearing. His name had to be written on everything. As I gathered things, I packed them into a suitcase that I had hidden in my closet, and crossed them off the list.

As Jeff and I continued to pray about this coming D-day, it was suggested by a close Christian friend that we send letters to friends and family who had a vested interested in Alex, explain our situation, and ask for financial support. This was a hard letter to write because I highly value our ability to provide for our family. Because I grew up without any money, being financially secure is an extremely important goal to me, but as I prayed about this, I could hear God telling me to give people a chance to be a part of this journey. In the end, we had many friends and family members who blessed us financially, and a few very special people who even supported us with a monthly donation. Every single dollar helped, but we were still left with providing the vast majority of the program fees on our own.

Although the financial part of this plan was concerning, the greatest stressor was how to get Alex to the ranch. I knew he would not go willingly. I had no idea how we would physically get our son, who played football as a defensive lineman, into our car and drive more than an hour away, when he did not want to go. Not only was the physical aspect of this daunting, but the emotional sickness that enveloped me every time I thought about how mad he would be, how hard he would argue, and how gut-wrenching it would be for me to hear him beg not to go, also caused me immense stress.

The plan was to enlist the help of several men from our church to physically escort Alex to the ranch. I knew it wouldn't be pretty, and his anger was going to be off the charts, but this was our only option.

Every day that I waited, the echoes of what Alex had told me after we took him to

Lincoln Prairie repeated in my head. "If you EVER send me away again, I will run away from you and NEVER EVER come back. You will NEVER see me again." The thought of this possibility coming true was terrifying; however, I decided that if this were the decision Alex made when all was said and done, at least he would be alive to make that decision. In the midst of this stress, however, there was a deep-seated peace. I had no doubt that Alex was supposed to go to this ranch. God had made it so clear. It was the burning bush I was asking Him for, and now all I had to do was keep my eyes on it.

Chapter Nine

It was about two weeks before Alex was to leave for the ranch, but I had no idea of the test that was coming for me. Alex was still neither going to school, nor coming home very often, but he had come home last night at one point and was asleep in his bed. I had stopped trying to wake him up for school. I was mentally and emotionally exhausted, and with the coming "D-day," I had decided not to fight with him about things I could ignore. So when I left for work that morning, I had only gone into his room to watch him sleeping, thankful that he was home and in his bed. At about 2p.m. that afternoon, Alex left me a voicemail.

"Hey, I just called because ummm if I texted you, I didn't know if you ummm would get it. I just woke up. I guess you didn't think I wanted to go to school, but I did. Ummm, I'm going to my friend's band practice in Virden. He's picking me up here in about a half hour- 45 minutes, ummm so maybe you'll be home, maybe you won't. I don't know. Give me a call back. I love you, bye."

This message was odd in that he had not been telling me anything for months about where he was going or what his plans were. There was something in his voice that was upbeat and sweet, and I can remember thinking how much I had missed this Alex.

Dinner was over before he came through our front door, and I was already into my night-time routine of choosing what I would wear to work the next day, cleaning my face, and flossing and brushing my teeth when he walked into my bedroom.

"How are you?" he asked me.

The question caught me off guard. I wasn't sure if he was just making pleasant conversation or if he really wanted to know. He looked tired, and his hair was longer than usual, but I couldn't help but feel a sense of joy that he had come into my room to talk to me. This had been such a normal everyday occurrence a year ago. Oh, how I missed my son.

As our conversation of pleasantries continued, I was walking around my room continuing my routine. I was in my closet selecting clothing, as Alex was leaning against my closet doorway.

"I don't want to run anymore, Mom." My breath was caught in my throat as I turned to face him.

"I'm tired. I miss my family. I need to get back into school and get caught up. I have to graduate, and I've missed a lot of school." Tears were building in his eyes as he looked at me, really looked at me, like he hadn't in almost a year. Words that I had been begging God for came tumbling out of Alex's mouth. I was stunned. Tears were streaming down my face. My heart was racing. I had no words. So instead, I wrapped him in my arms and held him, and we cried.

"Mom, I just want to be 16 again," he whispered in my ear.

"Alex, things have been totally out of control," I breathe, "but I want you home. I want you here, but you cannot have drugs in our home. I want you to get help, get back into school, and get things moving in the right direction. I miss you so much."

"I know. I have a lot of work to do, but I want to do it. I just want to be 16 again."

We talked for close to an hour before Alex left my room to take a shower. Left alone by myself, my mind was racing. Was this an act? Could Alex somehow know that his dad and I were about to whisk him off to the ranch? Was this just a coincidence? How could he know?

Was this genuine on his part? "God, I need your wisdom." Does Alex really want to get himself together, and 'be 16 again?' What do I do about the ranch? How can I send him now?"

I fell on my face and prayed with an intensity that was all encompassing. I was sobbing as I cried out to my Abba.

"Father, I KNOW you have told me to send Alex to this ranch. I have been praying for a clear sign, and you sent it. There is no question that you want us to send Alex there, and Lord I will obey what you have told me, even when it doesn't make sense. Why would Alex come to me now? Asking for help? Father, I'm so confused. How can I send him? Continue to make it clear what I am to do."

"DO YOU TRUST ME?" I heard echoing across the ticker of my mind. "DO YOU REALLY TRUST ME? I love Alex more than you can imagine, TRUST ME."

"Yes, Lord, I trust you."

As I continued to pray, my face on the floor, tears falling uncontrollably. I begged for wisdom and told God, once again, that I would do whatever it was He wanted me to do. I don't know how long I prayed or cried, but at some point I began recounting all the times God had shown Himself to me throughout this journey. There was no doubt that He was up to something. I had a rock-solid assurance in the very depths of my soul that Alex would be OK. I still had no idea when that would happen, but there was not a molecule of doubt in my mind. It was a strange sense of peace that I truly could not comprehend completely. The war for Alex's purpose on Earth was raging. Evil was tied around Alex's foot, trying to drag him down, but somehow, some way, I KNEW that God was going to use every single twist and turn for something amazing.

A thought bloomed.

Don't send Alex to the ranch.

Wait! What? Don't send Alex to the Ranch? This caught me completely off guard. An hour ago, there was NO QUESTION in my mind what God was telling me to do for Alex, and that was to send him to this ranch. However, this new thought about not sending Alex to the ranch was equally clear. I cannot explain it in any other way than to say it was also a directive from God.

In that moment, the story of Abraham and Isaac flashed through my mind. What on Earth could Abraham have been thinking when he heard God say, "Take your son, your only son, whom you love-Isaac-and go to the region of Moriah. Sacrifice him there as a burnt offering on a mountain I will show you."

His son, the one Abraham had prayed for, waited for, and had trusted God for was now being called by God to be a sacrifice? Abraham knew he had clearly heard the promises God had made to him. He knew what God was asking didn't make any sense, but because Abraham implicitly trusted God, he obeyed, and God did something amazing with Abraham's faith.

This was my Abraham moment. What I knew I was hearing from God did not make sense, but my trust in Him was unwavering. Even though it made no sense to me, and I had no proof that Alex would get his act together without some major intervention, I was going to trust God and let Him take us right up Mount Moriah.

Alex began attending school again and was focused on salvaging whatever grades he could before the end of first semester of his junior year. At night, he was sleeping at our house, and at least at first, it seemed that he was truly trying to change the trajectory of his life.

We spent Thanksgiving and Christmas surrounded by family, and although I was glad that Alex was a part of every celebration, there was something inside me that was hesitating to believe that the storm with Alex was over. And as 2012 began, it became apparent that Alex was only doing a better job of playing the game, trying to appear to be following what his dad and I required of him, while in reality he was still doing whatever he wanted to do.

"God, bring him back to you by any means necessary to get his attention." This type of surrender was frightening. I was giving permission to the God who parted the Red Sea, completely destroyed Sodom and Gomorrah, and allowed His own son to be brutally beaten and then crucified, to do whatever it took to reach my son. I knew that the love that God possessed for Alex was far beyond my comprehension. I knew that He only wanted what was best for Alex. I clung to that promise.

"But God, please, if possible, protect him from himself. Let him feel your love, God. I give him to you, God, because there is no more I can do."

Knowing that I still had no control over the choices he made, I chose to ignore what I could in exchange for peace. I was enjoying the evenness of my life with the absence of all the drama that the last 18 months had provided. The pressure in my chest had subsided, and all of a sudden, I was breathing without even thinking. I knew that Alex couldn't continue to be involved with the people he had been running with and actually become who he was supposed to be, but I also knew that God was quite capable of handling this situation all by Himself.

So, I continued to pray that God would get Alex's attention. I prayed that Alex would experience God in a way that he never had before. I prayed for Alex to make better choices, to be surrounded by healthy friends, to continue to go to school, and to become whole again.

Chapter Ten

Friday, February 24, 2012, began like any other morning. In fact, it had actually been a pretty good morning. Alex had been coming home by 9:00 p.m., and in return, he was able to drive to school. I knew he was still using; I just hoped that by our giving him the reward of driving to school that he would be encouraged. He had stopped running away. He was back in school. He was playing the game. Still doing what he wanted, but just not so "in our face" about it. I continued to pray.

That morning I arrived at school and had several chapters to cover with my students, but my classroom phone kept ringing. By the third call in less than 10 minutes, I rolled my eyes and walked over to the phone. As I picked up the receiver, I was stunned to hear the voice of Mrs. Poole, the assistant principal of Alex's school. She spoke words that brought my heart to a stop and my mind to a quick search for understanding.

"We have Alex in the office here. We found marijuana on him. He has been arrested. I thought you might like to be here when the police question him."

"Yes, I'll be right there," was all I could say.

I made my way to the back of my classroom and whispered to the other teacher the information I had just received. As I walked back to the front of the room, I noticed my hands were shaking. I stood in front of my students and told them I had a family emergency, and I had to leave. I could see the concern they wanted to express and the questions they wanted to ask on their faces, but no one said a word.

As I walked out of school, I phoned Jeff and explained what had happened.

"I need you." I told him. He agreed to meet me at the school.

In the car, I began to call my prayer warriors. Sherrie began praying immediately. My mom did the same. I drove with no radio, as I poured my heart out to God.

"God, this may have surprised me, but it did NOT surprise you. You were ready for this. I need you right now, God. Please be here. Let this be used to bring your glory. Bring him back, Lord. Please bring him back."

I pulled into a parking space in front of the school and just sat for a moment to gain my composure and say another prayer.

"Be here, God. Be here right in the middle of this." As I finished this prayer, I reached over and punched on the radio, and a blessed message spilled out.

"Hold fast, help is on the way. Hold fast, He's come to save the day."

I clicked the radio back off, and through my grateful, stunned tears, I smiled.

"I trust you, God. And even though I don't know where we will go from here, I trust that you do."

I entered the school. It felt as if every eye was trying not to look, but I saw looks that expressed embarrassment, disgust, shame, and curiosity come from every eye that caught mine. In this small school, word travels fast. It felt as if the whole school knew my heart was breaking, but was more interested in the gossip than helping me pick up the pieces.

I didn't even have to say whom I was when I walked into the office. The principal's office door was pulled open for me, and I walked through without saying a word, my eyes resting on Alex who was sitting at a round conference table.

The assistant principal caught me up on the details and showed me what was found, enough for a felony charge, we later learned. I saw a jar that I recognized sitting on the principal's desk filled with marijuana. It is a small, clear, glass, jelly jar that weeks ago held my mother's homemade apple butter. In the moment, my mind went to my mom, how much love she put into that jar, how disrespectful it felt to see the jar now filled with this substance that has caused so much pain. How could he use his grandmother's jar?

Jeff arrived, and we sat quietly at the round table with Alex. The police were searching Alex's locker and his car. They found nothing additional, which was irrelevant considering all that was already in their possession, several ounces of marijuana, some empty baggies, and a scale. The officer asked to speak to Jeff and me privately.

Once we were alone, he explained how much trouble Alex was in. The officer also explained how the juvenile system works. A minor in the state of Illinois must have 12 points to go to juvenile hall. He didn't think, since Alex had never been in trouble with the law, that he would be able to take Alex to juvenile hall right then, but he wanted to try to "put a scare into him." He told us he was going to handcuff Alex and put him into the police car while he waited for a call from the juvenile officer.

When the officer walked back into the office, Alex was still sitting at the table.

"Stand up and put your hands behind your back," he said to Alex.

Alex stood up, but said to the officer, "You can't give me the dignity of walking out of here without being handcuffed?"

"You lost that dignity when you decided to walk onto school grounds with drugs," the officer retorted.

Alex smirked, shook his head, and put his hands behind his back. The officer walked him through the halls and to a waiting cop car. After Alex's frame disappeared around the corner, the tears I had tried to hold back broke free. I apologized to the principal and Mrs. Poole for what Alex had done.

"I'm so sorry," I breathe.

"You don't need to be," her mouth said, but her body spoke differently.

After a short time, Alex was released to us. He received 9 points for this incident because it happened on school grounds, which was also the reason he would be charged with a felony. Since we had three cars at the school, Alex drove home. I followed him in my car. As I drove and cried, God watched and whispered, "I got this." Then it hit me, maybe this is why God told me to wait to send Alex to the Ranch just a few months ago. God was not surprised by what happened today. He knew what was coming. Maybe this was the answer we had been waiting for.

Chapter Eleven

Alex doesn't seem to be too worried, but I notice his words and his body don't agree. As I walk down our stairs to Alex's room, I pray for wisdom, and I pray for God to give me the right words to say.

"There's nothing to really say, Mom. I messed up," Alex says as he barely looks at me. I try to get a read on his eyes. There is a hint of fear, sorrowfulness, maybe a little indignation, and a regret that he disappointed me, but not enough for him to be broken.

"Alex, there is no place you can run where God can't find you. You've been trying to run from God, but He will never let you go. He is right beside you, just waiting for you to call out his name. There is nothing you can do to make God not love you. His mercy and grace are big enough to cover all of this."

"I hope so, Mom," he whispers.
As I fold him into my arms, I whisper to him that I KNOW that it is true and that I believe it with every fiber of my being.

"I hope so," he says again.

That night he goes out and gets high. He did this every night for the next two weeks. He stopped coming home on time, and didn't even come home some nights at all. I found out that he was hanging out with Wayne again. My heart raced with this information.

By Saturday morning, I had arranged a meeting with an attorney who came highly recommended by a friend who was himself a former judge. As Jeff, Alex, and I congregated outside an office building, we waited for the attorney to arrive. Once he arrived, we entered an elevator and made small talk on the way up to the fourth floor. I liked the no-nonsense talk of this guy. He didn't beat around the bush.

As Dan introduced himself, he told us that he worked with juveniles because they still had hope.

"There is still potential for their lives, and I like that. There isn't a whole lot of hope for most adults who are in the system, but kids? If we can just get their attention and get them to stop screwing up, we can change the trajectory of their lives. That's why I like working with adolescents."

He then turned his focus on Alex.

"You must stop the blood flow, here and now! Whatever you have been doing, STOP IT! If you get caught doing something else at this point, it will cause more pain and your parents more money."

I tried to quickly tell Alex's story, where we had been, how he came home in November and wanted to get himself together and back on track. How we almost sent him to a place called Salem Ranch just before Thanksgiving. This was the first Alex had heard of this, and I was curious about his thinking, but he did not react.

"The juvenile system, unlike the adult system, really is more interested in rehabilitation than punishment. It is possible that if you can get him into a program, the state's attorney might not press charges," Dan replied.

The possibility of this statement didn't really sink in because this entire meeting felt very surreal. Intellectually, I understood the ramifications of what a felony charge on Alex's record could mean, but at that moment I knew that he would never be charged and that the pieces were falling into place. How amazing! God KNEW that we would go through this, and He had already prepared a way for Alex to be healed of it all!!

In the next few days, as I discussed the Ranch as a possibility with Alex, I chose my words very carefully. I wanted to be merely a vessel that God used. The feeling that THIS was the answer to our present dilemma, as well as the on-going one, was budding inside me. It was a mixture of hope and dread, fear and faith, leaping and tip-toeing.

Alex repeatedly said that he would do whatever it took to not have a felony on his record. And as we sat at our kitchen table, I explained that his attorney wanted him to go to the Ranch, and furthermore, if he went, Dan thought there was a good chance that there would be no charges filed against him.

"Dan says that he cannot promise anything at this point," I tell Alex, but I already know what God's got planned.

"So, what is this program?" Alex asks.

"A horse ranch, where you go to school and have therapy, and work the ranch," I reply.

"How long do I have to be there?"

"Their shortest program is four months."

"What is the longest I'll be there?"

"Probably six months, but it depends on how well you work the program."

"Do I get to have visits?"

"There is no communication in the first six weeks, but after that you earn visits home. That is one of the cool things about this program; they work to reintegrate you back into your life. They don't just drop you as the last treatment center did."

After some silence, Alex replied, "If it will get rid of my felony, I'll go. But you need to understand that if I go and find out that I'm still getting charged, and you and Dad don't get me out of the program, I will run away, and you will never see me again." I looked into his eyes and said nothing.

Chapter Twelve

March 7, 2012

My feelings are a mixture of hope, dread, anticipation, sadness, ache, but mostly hope as we wait for Friday to arrive. I am not wanting Alex to go, but I want him back, which means he must go. It's a good thing that I know that God knows what he is doing. Good that His plan is better than any plan I could even dream. I don't have to worry whether this is the right decision. I know it is. I just want this to all be over, to be able to look back at it and see how it all happened, to see Alex being who he was created to be, not fighting and struggling, but peaceful, healthy, and whole again. His smile can surely light up a room.

"Blessed is the man who perseveres under trial, because when he has stood the test, he will receive the crown of life that God has promised to those who love him."

--James 1:12

March 10, 2012

We gave Alex to Salem Ranch yesterday. The day came early. By 5am, I was lying in bed thinking...waiting is so hard. God has shown me that His timing is perfect, but that doesn't change my human desire to have this all in the past. And yet I don't want to rush anything. I don't want Alex to become involved in the revolving door of rehab. I know God will use this time as an opportunity to change him from the inside. After all, that is the only place change happens.

"God, let him feel you, hear you. Without doubt, let your presence be known, so that Alex cannot deny you!"

It was a bright blue day with a chilly wind. I had been in dread for days knowing that Friday was coming. It wasn't that I questioned our decision, but I had such an immense feeling of sadness that we were at this place in Alex's life, on our road of parenting him. It was overwhelming sadness. Several times that day I just couldn't hold it together. I had to use all my power to keep myself composed, but I would find myself heaving with tears, gasping for air, and praying the only thing I could, "God, I need

you today. I need you. I need you. I need you."
And without hesitation, I heard a quiet, soft,
strong, "I know."

God was already there. Again, He knew
what I needed before I did. I am blown away by
His ever-presence. "Oh, how would I stand
today without you, God?"

Once we arrived at the Ranch, we were
given a tour, and after that was completed, we
found ourselves seated in a circle of chairs with
several workers from the Ranch. I kept praying
for God to be in that moment, to hold me
together. I couldn't fall apart in front of Alex. It
upsets him so when he sees me physically upset.
Ironic considering all the turmoil he has been the
cause of in the past 18 months. But on this day, I
needed to be strong. As the Ranch worker began
to question Alex about why he was there, I
waited anxiously to hear his reply.

"I'm trying to not get a felony on my
record."

"But what brought you here?" the worker
pushed.

"The wrong choices, I guess."

I could see the masked nervousness, the
apprehension of the unknown in his face, his
shoulders. It was almost as if he were trying to

nonverbally speak the words, "I might have to be here, but don't expect too much change from me. I'm just gonna do my time and then be on my way."

The worker turned to me, "Mom, what do you think are his issues?"

I slowly speak my assessment. Trying desperately to hold my emotion at bay. Another silent prayer, "Thy will be done. Thy will be done."

It is at this point that Alex learns that this is a Christian ranch. The workers assure Alex that he doesn't have to believe what they believe, but he will be required to attend certain "church" events. The anger in his eyes flashes at me, and I can see it wash over his entire body. I have intentionally not mentioned this to Alex because of his adamant rejection of God as of late. I was so thankful that it never came up in our conversations because I believe that would have been the one thing that would have caused him to refuse to come to the Ranch. God knew this too and had kept this fact from Alex until this moment, when there was no way he could run.

As the "meeting" concludes, we stand and are told to say our goodbyes. Alex is a conglomeration of varying emotions, but I pull him as close as he will let me.

"I love you," I whisper. "Please find what you need while you are here. Figure out how to come back from this. I miss you, and I want you back. I love you."

Alex is escorted through double glass doors. He turns and steals a glance at me as the doors to the outside world close behind him. Our eyes meet, but I pull away because that glance is connected to my very soul. He too is trying to hold it together; our bond is both an encouragement and a curse. In that one glance, so much isn't said.

The doors close as Alex walks away. I literally hold myself with my hands up on a table, trying to breathe, to not fall apart in front of these complete strangers. As I open my eyes, I am greeted by a promise from God that is sitting in a frame on the table:

"I am going to do something in your days that you would not believe even if you were told."
-- Habakkuk 1:5b.

This is another message to my heart from God. How can it be that, once again, God knows exactly what I need before I do? God has a plan for Alex. This I have never doubted! Something BIG, something spectacular, something that Alex was created specifically to do. And here in front of me was a physical reminder of this, a promise written in scripture. But even as this truth is sinking in, the pain and sadness that I have stuffed down all day erupts as I weep almost the entire trip home. I am, once again, thankful that Jeff is there to drive.

Chapter Thirteen

Six weeks have passed, and we will get to see Alex in three days. It has been a long, painful six weeks of waiting. But as I have waited, I have had no doubt that God is moving. I am so excited to learn where Alex is on this journey. What is he thinking? What has God already done? There is no question in my mind that God has been drawing Alex closer to Him. God has not had Alex for six weeks and done nothing! I am just so anxious to hear Alex tell of it!

I've prayed for Alex's heart to be softened, for God to show His love to Alex in a way that Alex has never before felt, in a way that Alex has no chance of denying. I have asked for Alex to feel that he is being wrapped up in the arms of God and covered by His mercy and grace. "God, be REAL to him!!"

We have a decision to make: Doug, Alex's therapist, phoned tonight to discuss how this weekend would work. There is no place at the Ranch for us to stay; someone had already reserved the apartment. Jeff and I had planned to stay in a hotel in Bloomington for the weekend, but we are having a hard time finding a suitable room for us and two teenage boys. Either there are none available or the one hotel we found was prohibitively expensive. The other choice is to bring him home.

"Alex would be disappointed if he didn't get to come home for his visit, but he knows that it probably isn't going to happen," Doug shares.

Guilt followed by fear washes over me. I'm sure Alex wants to sleep in his own bed, see our dog, Shadow, and our cat, Conrad, just be home, but will he sneak out? Will friends sneak in? Will we fight about his not getting to be with friends? Will he get his phone, X-box, and computer back? If so, we can't control who knows he is home. As I explained this to Doug, he assures me that all this is normal and that he doesn't foresee any major problems with Alex. But I still do not know what decision is right.

After explaining everything to Jeff, we both decide to pray about it and talk tomorrow. So, I begin to pray.

"Lord, I'm needing help with this one. Is it too soon to bring him home? You know where he is, God. Help me to make the right decision, to do what is best for Alex. I need a burning bush, God. Make it obvious, so I can't miss it."

Then in a small whisper I pray, "Give Jeff a strong feeling, and I'll know it is you."

The next morning Jeff says we should bring Alex home. I don't think it is the right thing to do, but I am going to trust this is from God.

Chapter Fourteen

I haven't slept well for the last couple of nights. I'm anxious and excited about seeing Alex today. I wake early, and as I am still lying in my bed, I am praying.

"I get to see my baby today! Oh, Father! Be with us. I know that you have not had this boy for six weeks and done nothing with him. God, make your power evident! I know that he is going to be in such a different place. Let this be a peaceful, positive time together."

The day goes slowly, but I will myself to suppress the bubbling excitement and nervous questioning in my mind. Will he still be angry? Will he go to church with us on Sunday? Will he want to run with his friends? Will he be glad we sent him? Will he and God have figured some things out?

As Jeff and I drive for the next hour and 45 minutes, our conversation is easy. We discuss how we think the events of the weekend will go and our nervousness about seeing Alex. I'm praying constantly, talking to God, praising what I'm sure He has already done.

A song by Jamie Grace that I have felt strong connection to throughout this time hums in my head: *"You lead, I'll follow. Your hands are my tomorrow. Your grip, your grace; you know you've got me tenderly. You lead. I'll follow. Just light the way, and I will follow 'cause I know what you've got for me is more than I can see. So, lead me on!"*

I ask Jeff if we can pray together, just as we are about to turn on the road that leads to Salem Ranch. I pray out loud because I believe there is POWER in the spoken word.

"God be with us. You know where we are right now. Please help us to have the right words, to be patient, to enjoy each other this weekend. Lord, we thank you for what we KNOW you have already done. Help us, Amen."

I think Alex sees me before I see him because he is walking to the door at the same time as I am. The light is back in his eyes. The sadness, at first glance, appears to be gone. The anger has disappeared from his shoulders. His hair is much shorter. I like it. It lets his beautiful brown eyes and magnificent smile light up the room again. We embrace, and I can feel the heat of his body, as I hold my baby in my arms. He is alive. He is here. Everything is going to be O.K.

For the next several hours, Alex talks about everything: the horse, picking stalls, chores, the boys at the Ranch, the staff, the food, the beds (he needs a different pillow) and his roommate, Michah. Alex's statement about Michah is the clue I've been searching for.

"He's not a bad kid. He just got away from God for a while," Alex chatters away.

That was all I needed to hear. All I needed to know was that God had indeed been softening his heart. He'd been working on Alex. I almost couldn't hold back my tears. Alex was speaking as if he not only believed in the mercy of God, but as if he were also recognizing it in other people too. More proof came as Alex and I discussed what he had gone through over the past six weeks.

"Anything else you want to ask me about?" Alex asks.

"What about church?"

"I was so mad at you when I found out this was a Christian facility. I never would have come, judging from where I was six weeks ago, if I had known. You didn't tell me!"

"You didn't ask."

"I know," Alex smirked.

"I cannot believe you didn't Google the Ranch to check it out."

"I can't either."

"The list of things you had to take, had a Bible listed on it, but you never looked at it. You wanted me to pack, so you had no idea what was on that list," I said shaking my head in amazement.

"There were just too many 'coincidences' for this to not have been God, Mom. I know I am where I am supposed to be. One of the reasons I think I was sent to Salem is because I think I'm going to end up working there one day."

My stunned heart could almost not take all that was coming from my son, who just eight weeks ago was saying things like "your God" and "your faith" and wouldn't even acknowledge (and tried to deny) God's very existence. He now thinks he might work at a CHRISTIAN facility for troubled boys?!

"Is this what this entire journey was about, God? That Alex would come to this place in order to serve you? God, you are good. I stand in awe of your power, love, and mercy."

"In this you greatly rejoice, though now for a little while you may have had to suffer grief in all kinds of trials. These have come so that your faith of greater worth than gold, which perishes even though refined by fire, may be proved genuine and may result in praise, glory and honor when Jesus Christ is revealed."   --1Peter 1:6-7

Chapter Fifteen

We are waiting on a phone call from Alex. He has been back at the Ranch for a few weeks since his first visit home. His new counselor, Nicole, told me that Alex would call at 7 p.m., so we waited. I felt like a schoolgirl waiting for the phone to ring, anticipating hearing the sound of that really cute boy saying, "Hello" on the other end when I answered. I checked twice to be sure that my ringer was on. I didn't move from a room without my phone.

At 6:50 p.m. we sat down to eat dinner, figuring Alex would interrupt us as we ate. But 7 p.m. came and went and no call. By 7:30 p.m., he still hadn't called, and I began to hypothesize about why. Yes, he was calling after 8 p.m., as I had asked him to in my letter. That must be what was going on. But at 8:15 p.m., there was still no call, and Jeff had to leave for his softball game.

"Tell Alex, 'Hi!' for me," he said as he kissed me goodbye.

At 8:30 p.m., I'm getting concerned and check my phone again. At 8:40 p.m., I have a sinking feeling that he won't be calling, and I try to busy myself. At 8:45 p.m., my phone rings. Even though I'm confused by the number on my screen, I quickly answer it, thinking it MUST be Alex!

My heart sinks to my stomach, as Nicole explains that Alex was heard by staff cussing in the kitchen after dinner. And because of this, he will not be calling. But even worse, he will lose his home visit for the weekend, which includes Mother's Day.

"Alex didn't take it very well. He said he will speak with Mike, the director, in the morning and is pretty confident that Mike will remove the punishment. I will let you know if I hear anything else. I'm sorry," Nicole says with genuine sympathy.

A familiar feeling of sadness rushes over me, and as tears pour down my face, I begin to pray.

"God, let Alex be wise. Let him receive justice. Let him not be so angry or upset that he goes in the wrong direction. And God, please help me too. I miss him."

It is in that moment that I remember, I will get to see Alex on Saturday at his track meet. Even though I want him home on Sunday, as least we can spend Saturday together. I am comforted by this thought. The next morning, I send Nicole an email to verify that Alex will still be at the track meet.

"No. I'm sorry. The boys cannot participate in sports when they are on Punishment Packet," is the reply I receive. I sit in my car and cry like a baby.

June 22, 2012

A few weeks later, Alex was asked by a leader at the Ranch to give some "investors" a tour of the ranch. Alex really enjoyed the opportunity to show people around and said that he would be getting more chances to do this. He also was given an opportunity to go to a Kiwanis meeting to share what his experience at the ranch has been like. Alex really enjoyed doing this and said that he would be able to go to more places to share his story. I am watching the most beautiful miracle unfold!

I am overwhelmed with gratitude. How is it that the God of the universe has heard me? Has answered *my* prayers? Who am I to deserve such love, grace, and mercy? The changes in Alex are nothing short of a work of God, an undeniable miracle, and I have been witness to it all. "Oh! God, how do I ever repay you? You have rescued Alex from such bondage. You have given him a clean slate. You have shown yourself to him in a way that he has never experienced. You have done everything for which I have prayed. Everything I knew, believed, hoped, clung to, and fought for is all happening right before my very eyes. I am before my King prostrate. I am so unworthy, and yet you hear every whisper deep in my soul. Lord of all creation, of water, Earth, and sky, you are holy!"

July 3, 2012

Today Alex had an MRI for his shoulder. We had to be at the doctor's office by 7:30 a.m. His appointment began at 8 a.m., and it took about an hour. He had nerve testing at 10 a.m., so we went to breakfast in between. After the waitress brought our food, Alex reached across the table for my hand and asked, "You wanna pray?" So there, in the middle of Denny's restaurant, we bowed our heads and he prayed…another moment in my miracle, another opportunity to praise God for being so faithful.

I'm bursting at the seams wanting to share how God is making Alex whole and answering my prayers. Every time I start to say that what is happening is unbelievable so beyond what I dreamt, I have to stop because it is not. God is and has been reading my heart. He knew my sincerest, deepest dreams for Alex, and these are being realized because my hope has always been that Alex would seek God. That he would experience God like never before, follow Him and use this entire experience to bring glory to the power of mercy and grace through salvation through Christ.

I never doubted for one moment that we would get to this point with Alex. What I am overwhelmed by and what has simply consumed me is thankfulness. Knowing that God is faithful. Knowing that He will make everything right is a completely different experience than getting to watch it with your own eyes. How do I explain the majesty I am engulfed in? I feel a constant sense of joy, even on the days when I am frustrated about something insignificant like too much to do, not enough time, or rude people in a store, or careless drivers or the highway. I am so quickly reminded that none of that matters. Who am I to feel and harbor frustration when so many times God has been frustrated with me? Yes, forgiveness is all I find when I turn to him.

I find myself holding on to stuff less and less, things like my anger, frustration, impatience. I constantly listen to Christian music either on the radio or on CDs. This is the backdrop of my day, and I am amazed that at any moment my casual listening will turn into genuine praise. I might be putting on my makeup and stop because I need to raise my hands and sing "How Great is our God." Or I might be driving down the road and feel the urge to reach out to God because I know "Healing Rain" is falling down on Alex, and I need to tell God "Thank You." Or songs that got me through some of the darkest hour play, and I am reminded of what God has brought me through. If our God is for us, who can be against us?

God has used other people's experiences to encourage me, to sustain me, to help me to cling to his promises. I have to say that this experience with Alex has been the first time in my life when I have had unshakeable faith. I am not bragging, but it is true and honestly a new place in my walk with God. I NEVER doubted for one moment that God would bring Alex back, that God would take this experience and use it and that God would be glorified in a BIG way. With every twist and turn, scary moment, bad choice, heartbroken tear, I knew God was right there watching everything, whispering, "I've got this, don't be afraid, I've got this, trust me." I felt this truth in the core of the fibers of my being. It is the most remarkable feeling to *know* beyond any doubt that the God of the universe is holding your dreams in His hands. But then to get to SEE the proof of this power-all I can say is, "WOW GOD!!"

"Truly I say to you, whoever says to this mountain, 'Be taken up and thrown into the sea,' and does not doubt in his heart, but believes that what he says will come to pass, it will be done for him. Therefore, I tell you, whatever you ask in prayer, believe that you have received it, and it will be yours."   --Mark 11:23-24.

July 14, 2012

I talked with Alex on Thursday of this week. He was very upbeat. He had gone to speak to another group about Salem. He said it was a group of about 50-60 people. He talked about his passion to get our church involved with Salem because he knew our church was "all about helping and reaching out to people."

July 22, 2012

Alex was home for a week visit, and he went to church with us today. I'm thankful for the welcome he received! Hugs, kind words, and shared prayers were all around him. The greatest part of today was that Alex and Tom, our youth pastor, not only spoke to each other, but there was also an embrace that left me thankful. As the memories of the anger and betrayal Alex and Tom had exchanged, came flooding back to me, I had a hard time keeping it together in church. I knew this was a moment of healing for Alex. Forgiveness was in that hug. Alex and Tom have made plans to have lunch on Tuesday, another opportunity for wounds to heal.

July 24, 2012

I have noticed images of pot leaves and messages such as "Legalize Now," "I Love Pot" on Alex's computer since the last several visits. I checked his Facebook and even on the public view, there are several references to pot and a couple of "f" words. Other red flags have gone up too; his almost paranoid angry admission that he "doesn't like to call himself a 'Christian' because of crazy people who do things like the Westboro Baptist Church.'"

Our youth pastor, Tom, cancelled lunch today. We spoke on the phone as he explained that he just wasn't ready to meet with Alex, although, he didn't tell Alex that. The cancelling of this lunch was quite significant, and I had believed, offered an opportunity for Alex to grow. When I first saw all the drug references on Alex's social media, and then heard from Tom, I was an emotional mess; panic, fear, and doubt washed over me. As I began to pray, I simply told God that I didn't know what to say, but that I needed him. I didn't know what to say to Alex. However, I knew that not only did I have to talk to him, but that I also was so transparent that I knew Alex would know something was wrong. I called Sherrie, one of my close friends and prayer warriors. While still on the phone, she prayed with me in the parking lot of Shop-N-Save. I drove home still talking to God, and he quickly reminded me that so many good things had taken place in Alex's life over the last five months. Alex was listening to God now, and that HE was still in control. I didn't see this as a set back but as a moment to know the truth. Alex was a work in progress. These areas were things he still needed to work on, in order to become who God wanted him to be. These things becoming an issue or getting brought to the forefront were God's way of making sure that Alex couldn't fake it or hide or ignore it, and that I wouldn't be fooled into thinking he was completely healthy. God's timing was perfect, as always, because as Alex moved into Phase 3 at the ranch, the ranch began a sanding process with his character. The real issues began to be dealt with so that he would resemble God's creation more and more.

Chapter Sixteen

Oct. 4, 2012

And then Alex was home. Seven months to the day, life at Salem Youth Ranch was over for Alex. I can't say that I was overjoyed that this moment was here. Oh, I wanted to be, but the fear and uncertainty of what would happen was all encompassing. Would Alex follow our rules now that the threat of the Ranch was gone, or would he slowly digress into habits from before? Yet again, I needed God's peace to engulf me, to cover me, to remind me that HE was in control and all my worrying couldn't change that. Time would be my proof that the changes Alex said he had made were real. My heart wanted to believe, but my head wouldn't stop chattering about all the potential pit falls.

November 2012

Today Alex has been home for a month. He has finished another class toward his graduation. Only two more to go! He has a job at Schnucks grocery store, he has registered for classes in the spring at LLCC, and I am happy to say is a changed person. With each passing day and every time he does what he is supposed to do: comes home on time, calls to inform me where he's going, does not come home smelling like pot or alcohol. I am more and more at ease. I sleep slightly better each night. However, I do have to admit that the scars from the pain of fear are still very tender. It doesn't take much of a hit to make them throb with intensity again. I'm amazed at how I can be physically overcome by these all too familiar feelings of churning in my chest, tightness in my ribs, and panic in my soul. At those moments, I have to remember to pray for God's presence. HE is my rock.

To my surprise, Alex came home one day and said he wanted to apply to Greenville College, a small private Christian college just an hour or so from home. I was thrilled with this news. We got busy and completed the necessary application and financial aid paperwork. He planned to start classes in January 2013.

December 31, 2012

Alex left for the Passion Conference today. I have prayed for this day for months. This conference brings together thousands of college students from across the country to experience God together through music, teaching, and fellowship. I KNOW God is going to do amazing things! From the moment Alex decided to go, about five months ago, I KNEW God had a plan.

This morning his alarm was going off and his door was locked. He had left through the window and not come home. My first thought was panic. I was afraid that Jeff's fear that at the last-minute Alex wouldn't go would come true. I started praying immediately. Alex answered his phone and said that he had fallen asleep at a friend's house but would be home in 15 minutes. I must admit, those were a long 15 minutes! But he got here, got packed, and we left for the church on time. I told him as we drove that I had been praying for him, that I knew God had big plans for him, and that I just wanted him to be open to whatever God wanted for his life.

As we got out of the SUV, unloaded his bags, and reloaded them into one of the three long white vans, I felt nervous for him. Knowing that this was the first time he was walking into a group of kids who knew exactly what he had done, who know what he was before.

He didn't want me to go into the church with him. As I drove off, he slung his backpack over his shoulder, and walked through the glass doors of the church. I cried out as I drove away, "God, let those kids be Christ-like. Let them love Alex, show him mercy and show him grace. Let Alex experience you in a way he never has before. Let him be open to you and what you want to do with him. Empty him out, Lord. Remove ALL desire for ungodly things. Let him turn his entire life over to you."

January 3, 2013

It has been a quite week. I've prayed continually, as have Sherrie, Mom, Angie, and Debbie. I know God is working, even though all I hear right now is silence. There is no indication from Alex about what is going on around him, inside of him. I so want to watch it, but I know God's busy even though I hear no commotion. Alex comes home in two days, and I am anxious to know what has transpired.

January 5, 2013

I wake up to the following post on Facebook from Alex:

I am overjoyed by God's goodness! How can it be that He continues to be so faithful to us?!!

Alex will be home later today, and my excitement to hear about his experience is increased by this post.

A few hours later, Alex came home from the conference, dropped his bags, took off his shoes, then went to his room and to the garage. He, then, walked back to the front door and put his shoes on. I tried to hug him and talk to him about his FB post.

"You can't hug me yet."

"What are you doing?"

"I'm going across the street."

"To do what?"

"If you watch me, you will see!"

As I watched, he tramped through the snow to the overgrown drainage ditch at the end of our street, and began throwing things into the weeds. Throwing them as far and as hard as he could. He shook out a bag, chucked something small, threw things on the ground, smashed things on the concrete, kicked, and stomped. He was destroying his stash of drugs and various paraphernalia that he had had hidden, unbeknownst to us, in our home. Then he turned and walked back to our house. He stepped in and stood in our front entryway and said,

"Now you can hug me." For a long time, we did. We hugged like we hadn't seen each other in years and sobbed.

"I'm so sorry it has taken me so long," Alex said through his tears.

"It doesn't matter now."

"I know, but I still want to say it. I'm so sorry."

"I know," I whispered as tears of thankfulness overtook me.

Chapter Seventeen

January 6, 2013

Today, Alex came to talk to our small group at church and the Sunday school class that had financially supported him at Salem. He was so brave and just radiated the Grace of God! I was proud, touched, amazed, and thankful all at once. He spoke with a deep, quiet, confident voice. He told those people how grateful he was for their support. How he couldn't have gotten where he was without them. He apologized for not coming to talk to them sooner, but confessed that he didn't want to come and lie to them to tell them that he was doing great, when he was still using every day. They asked if they could pray for him, and as Alex and I stood in the middle, 20-30 people laid hands on us and prayed.

Later that morning, I watched as Alex praised God in church, raising his hands. I could see his fire! I kept sneaking peeks to see what he was doing. He and a friend were standing side by side with hands raised. WOW! What a power I was witnessing.

January 7, 2013

Alex received an email from Greenville College today; it was his financial aid packet information. He was awarded over $7,000 in scholarships! How great is our God?! It is funny because I am thrilled, but not surprised! I KNEW that God would provide in a big way, and He did. It is also funny that when you tell God your deepest wish, He hears you. Sometimes He says, "No," but he always hears your heart's desire. I had told Alex that if we get half of his school paid for with scholarships, we would be OK. Guess how much his scholarship money was? ALMOST exactly one-half.

"Thank you, God, for heaping blessings upon us! I have never doubted your plan or your ability to take this mess and make something beautiful. But what a marvel it is, though, to be watching it all unfold. Thank you for your perfect timing and wisdom!"

Weeks pass as we prepare Alex to leave for school. The day before he is to leave, there is still so much to be packed. As I was dragging out pairs of pants and folded socks, I was reminded of all the times when he was little that I packed him up for a night sleepover. I am a mixed bag of emotions tonight. I am so thankful that we are where we are. After all, we raised him hoping he would go off to college, but I cannot help but wish he were little again, and I was packing for just a night. My baby is grown. There were moments when I thought we'd never reach this day, and moments when I can't believe 17 years have actually come and gone. This life really is fleeting. I am struck by how we only get one shot at some things in life, and raising our children is one of them.

"God, protect him. Keep him on your path. Provide strong Christian friends who will guide him, build him up, and give him success at Greenville."

On January 25, 2013, 5 a.m. came early. My excitement was tempered by my anxiety. As we loaded the car with Alex's final things, I couldn't help but be thrown back to a morning almost a year ago. A morning I thought I might not be able to hold myself together. A morning that was filled with obedience to God and fueled by my undying love for a lost son who WOULD find his way back, even if I died in the process. Today was not that day! Today was a day to rejoice for all the blessings God had bestowed on us and for His faithfulness.

When we arrived at Greenville, we were greeted by a young man named Travis. He had plugs in his ears, a bearded face, and a friendly warm smile. We had to carry Alex's things to the fourth floor, but we were met by offers to help as we climbed each step. Each person we met greeted Alex with a smiling welcome, followed by a handshake and an introduction.

"Hey, you must be the new guy. I'm…"

"Hi! I'm…welcome to Joy Hall."

"Hey, are you Alex? I'm … you are gonna love it here. This is the best hall and floor on campus!"

A note, taped to Alex's dorm room, echoed those same sentiments. Alex was receiving a marvelous welcome! As Jeff, Alex, and I emptied bags and organized Alex's things, some of the other boys who lived on Joy 4th stood in the doorway and chatted. Tyler Wright, a student we had met on our visit to campus a few weeks back, appeared to say, "Hi" and welcomed, Alex.

After some direction from several of the other students, Jeff, Alex, and I set out across campus to finish necessary paperwork at the security office before the orientation began. We spent the day helping and watching Alex learn how to slip into this new role as a college student.

When the time came to say goodbye, I felt such a sense of peace. After all this time, Alex wanted to be here. This time we could talk whenever we wanted or needed. This time Alex was welcoming God into His rightful position. As I held my son, the college student, for a long time, I began to feel such a sense of relief. He WAS HERE! Where I had only dreamed he'd be. Actually, my dream wasn't as amazing because I never dreamt of a Christian school for him; that is all further evidence of the GREATNESS of God!

The scenery sped by as Jeff drove our now empty SUV home. Now the tears came. I wept because I couldn't believe all we had been through; the long, terrifying, painful, gut-wrenching experience that we had gone through. So many nights of screaming out to God, begging for a miracle, begging for Him to save my son. Many nights of not knowing where Alex was, or when or if he'd come home. It all ended here. How overcome with gratitude I found myself!

"Thank you, God. Thank you, God. You are the King of the Universe! Why you take notice of me and why you have shown your love, mercy and grace on my son, I'll never completely understand. But I just want to say thank you!"

Chapter Eighteen

February 5, 2013

Just a couple of weeks later, Alex is having a really hard time adjusting. He is depressed, anxious, overwhelmed. He is questioning why he is there. I am trying so hard to encourage him, to help him understand that most kids have a hard time adjusting to college, that he has been through so much, and he needs to trust that God has a plan.

He says some things that scare me. Off the wall stuff like he wants to get off his depression meds because "after all they are witchcraft anyway." I just pray when things like this come out of his mouth. I must give it to God, and I have to remind myself of this every day because I keep wanting to take it back, even though I know that God is, will be, and has been faithful. I know that HE has such a glorious plan for Alex.

"God, show Alex that he belongs. Give him confidence, lessen his anxiety, send godly people to surround him."

February 5, 2013

As I am scrolling through Facebook, I see the following post from Alex:

Now I know why I chose to do drugs every day for two years.

This comment brought a cascade of encouraging words from people.

"God is good."

"Bro, I'm coming over."

I immediately send out a "We need prayer" text and begin to pray like crazy. I texted Alex scripture and prayed some more. Before he went to bed, Alex texted me that my prayers had helped and that his friend Tyler had come over to talk and pray and that had helped a lot too.

"Oh, Lord. Once again, I ask you to surround my boy with your love. Let him see you; feel your presence. Holy Spirit, protect him. Let him know why you have him there-that this is part of your plan." Before I turned out my lights, I prayed for myself as well. I prayed for peace and that God would allow sleep to wash over Alex and me.

I woke up the next morning with a new energy. I prayed for Alex all day that God would show him that he belongs at Greenville. Later that day at 4:30, Alex texted me:

`I got a job LOL`

What an answer to prayer!! A total God thing!!

A few days later, Jeff and I got to visit Alex, have lunch, and explore the town of Greenville a bit. As we checked out a local furniture re-sale shop, Alex immediately hit it off with the owner. She talked to Alex for the entire 45 minutes we were there. I don't think she took a breath! But in the end, Alex asked if she might need help every now and then. She told him that "they" had just started discussing that "they" might want to hire someone every now that then. She asked Alex to bring his school schedule, so she could look at it. A few days later, he did just that and was hired as the first non-family member to ever to work in their family-owned shop. As the owner's daughter explained that his school came first and to never be afraid to tell them no when they called if he had homework, Alex seemed encouraged. Once again God had been faithful. This was no coincidence; it was a God plant!

February 24, 2013

Jeff, Drew, and I met Alex and James, Alex's new friend from school, in Collinsville. We ate a late lunch, and then headed to the Scott Trade Center in St. Louis for The Winter Jam 2013. The concert had no ticket seating, which ended up being pretty frustrating and chaotic. As we attempted to find seats, I could especially feel the anger and irritation building in Alex. There were people everywhere. Every time we entered a small section of seating, we found no seats available. By the time we finally found seats for all five of us, Alex was grumbling, even cussing under his breath.

"We should just go," Alex said more to himself than to me.

The entire time I was praying. I prayed that we'd find seats, but I mostly prayed that God would speak.

"Father, please speak to each of us. Please send each of us a message that is specifically tailored, so we will hear what we need to hear."

As the concert began, I watched Alex's irritation slowly melt until he was standing and singing with his arms raised. Song after song, I watched him. I was once again overwhelmed to watch this experience with God unfold. I began to think about how far we had come, from a complete denial that God existed, to a complete surrender to his will. My emotion wasn't containable. I stood in a crowd of 20,000 people and cried with my hands raised to my God, my savior. "Thank you for this miracle."

Chapter Nineteen

March 4, 2013

The last few days Alex has been sick. He had the flu starting on Thursday night, and he got really sick on Friday. I got a text from him several days ago saying he was so worn out, and he did not know he was going to be able to keep going forward. I started praying like crazy for him. I felt a serious hopelessness in his voice, and I sent out a text message to my prayer warriors asking them to pray like crazy.

This morning I got a text message from Alex:

I can't do this. I can't. I'm done.

I immediately called Alex and prayed with him on the phone. He wept. He had stopped taking his depression medicine. He told me that he had been trying to wean himself off it and was now really suffering the full emotional effects. He was clearly in a state of serious depression.

I decided to drive to Greenville. When I got there, we talked for quite awhile. There were times when he said things that really scared me. He told me that he had a dream that Satan was talking to him. He felt bound, like he couldn't move, like he was trapped. I felt strongly that was exactly what was happening. Satan was trying to bind him, to lock him down, entrap him and not let the amazing things that God had planned for him to transpire. But, I KNEW the power of God was so much bigger than that!

An hour or so later, Alex and I met with an advisor on campus named Fallon. When we first got there, Alex started discussing what he was dealing with. He broke down pretty quickly and began crying.

"I don't want to let you down, Mom. I know you have done so much for me. I just don't want to let you down."

"You aren't letting me down, Alex. College is a big adjustment. I'm so proud of you already, just for being here, for trying to do this. You've come so far."

Fallon was able to give Alex some great ideas on how to get himself back on track. She also said she would connect him with a couple of people who could help him with studying. We left Fallon's office and headed for a place to eat dinner. There aren't many choices in Greenville, but we chose a family restaurant, just outside of campus which was by the interstate. We went in and sat down, got his books out, and started working. We weren't working very long before this man walked by and saw my Lanphier High School sweatshirt.

"I went to Southeast High School. What year did you graduate from Lanphier," he said.

"Oh, no, no, I don't go to school there. I work there. I am a teacher."

"Really?! My dad taught at Southeast High School for 25 years."

We made a little more small-talk until our waitress brought the food Alex and I had ordered. The man stepped back and took a seat at a table next to Alex and me. Alex and I bowed our heads, held hands across the table, and prayed before we began eating.

Within a few moments, the man began to have a conversation with us. I'm embarrassed to admit that I was a little irritated. Alex and I had planned to sit there and work on homework, and now this stranger was messing up the plan. But as the conversation continued, I could hear God telling me to let it go.

"God knows about this," I whispered across the table to Alex.

Alex shook his head and closed his book. It became quickly apparent to me that this stranger was a God plant. His name was Keith. He was really friendly. He was a bus driver now, but a retired farmer who had farmed with his dad for 36 years. He talked about losing his dad, that you don't get it to do over again, and how the world was lost without Christ. He talked about that when you think you can't go any further, all you have to do is call out, and God will be right there for you. He said that it was good to have your mom, but it was even better to have God on your side. As we listened and the man spoke, I couldn't help but be amazed at how this was another one of those moments where God made sure that Alex knew that He was right there with him.

The man told us the story of his dad dying. He got a phone call from the EMT who was driving the ambulance. The driver knew Keith personally and said they had his mom and dad. There was some confusion about who was in the ambulance. The gentleman thought that his mother, who is diabetic, was in the ambulance and that his father was following behind in the car, but the opposite was just true. Before Keith could even get to the hospital, his father had passed. He described what a close relationship he had with his dad after farming side-by-side for 36 years.

This man then asked if we knew the song by Mercy Me, *I Can Only Imagine.* He continued to tell us that he knew his dad was at home in Heaven and that someday, he would get to see him again. He said that he felt the Holy Spirit around him when his dad died, almost like it was his dad standing right beside him.

Alex and I exchanged glances, of course, many times as this gentleman, Keith, spoke. He and I were both thinking the same thing; we knew this was God. This was God making sure that Alex knew He was right there. So, we parted ways and told this complete stranger, that no longer felt like a stranger, we wished him well. We walked then to the parking lot and got into our SUV.

"And you doubt that God knows where you are?" I said, as we pulled out of the restaurant parking lot.

Alex smiled and shook his head. At that moment, we both realized the song on the radio was *This is the Stuff You Use,* by Francesca Battistelli, and we both had a little chuckle. The very next song was Mercy Me's, *I Can Only*

Imagine. At first, Alex and I just laughed because it was just like, "Oh, my gosh, God! Are you serious? Really?" I was just overwhelmed because God, once again, showed me that He was there and that He was listening, that He cared so much; I am overwhelmed by God. I'm overwhelmed by his good, perfect plan. I'm overwhelmed that He listens to me. He listens to *me.* I don't deserve it, but He does.

We got back to campus, and Alex and I immediately went to the library and got started on the homework. He and I were able to complete almost the entire study guide for his big Western Civilization test that was causing him a lot of stress. We worked as long as we could together before he had to be at a study session.

I am so thankful that today was Casimir Pulaski Day and that I could go and be with Alex. He needed me today, not just as his mom, but also as a guide to continue to show him the love of Christ.

"I know something big is happening here God. I am so honored. I'm just so honored to be a part of it. Thank you, God. Thank you, God. Thank you, God."

Chapter Twenty

By May, Alex was home and had successfully completed his first semester of college. However, the summer I had expected did not materialize. At 5:15 a.m. on May 25, 2013, Alex came home drunk. He stumbled out of a sad white car that stopped in front of our house. I watched his legs wobble under him, as if they belonged to a newborn colt, as he walked up the driveway. I found him huddled in a corner relieving himself near our fence, cigarette in hand.

"You're drunk."

"Um, yeah, sorry," was his reply.

I knew this moment was not the time to discuss anything, so I continued my normal morning routine. As I worked out, Alex messed around in the bathroom and kitchen trying to make small talk with me. I silently prayed for wisdom and words. Nothing really came. When he finally went to lie down, he hugged me and told me he loved me. I continued to pray all day for God to help me not want to fix it or even feel that I had to.

Around 2:00 p.m., I slipped home to deposit groceries I had purchased over my lunch. To my surprise, the SUV and Alex were gone. I called him, and he answered right away.

"Where are you?"

"I lost my phone. I've been looking everywhere. I finally found it at Bradley's house."

"OK. You heading home?"

"Drew wants me to pick him up from school. I'll be home after that."

"Don't forget, we are having dinner to celebrate Dad's birthday tonight."

"I know. I'll be there."

Alex didn't show for dinner; at 8:30 p.m., he finally texted:

```
I'm sorry.  I'm staying at
Bradley's tonight.
```

For the next 12 hours, he ignored my calls, texts, and pleas to bring home the SUV. If he was not in a condition to drive, I asked him to tell me where the SUV was, and I would come pick it up. He never responded, and hours later, still no SUV.

About 8:30 a.m. the next morning, I found my wallet open and a small, silver, metal-cross which is always in my change compartment, lying inside my purse. I then looked outside and noticed my mailbox and beautiful purple clematis, which was in full glorious bloom, were gone. Flowers were shredded on the grass, but the entire mailbox was gone. As I looked further down the street, I saw the SUV and began to walk toward it. Alex had already placed the mailbox in the trunk. He was lying on the concrete on his side, pulling bright purple blooms, entangled in wire, from underneath the vehicle. Obviously drunk, slurring his words, wobbly legs, cigarette in hand, he was indignant that I was blaming him and incredulous about my saying he was drunk.

Jeff was able to dislodge the now ball of metal and flowers from under the car. Thankfully, our neighbor had already taken the keys from Alex. While all this was happening, a friend of Alex's was sitting in our SUV. I yelled at him and told him to get out of our car.

Alex cussed and mumbled as he and his friend stumbled down the sidewalk. The SUV was obviously the party vehicle for the night: a girl's purse, bag of tortilla chips, a half-melted container of ice cream, a Garfield book, bottle of unopened wine (which I promptly emptied down the drain), and two debit cards were littered throughout. A broken sissy handle, the driver's side headrest, a mailbox and a breathtakingly beautiful clematis bush were the casualties of the night.

When I came back in the house, I looked closer at my wallet and discovered that about $70 was missing. I immediately called Alex, and he denied it. Jeff, furious at this point, took off down the street to chase Alex down. When Jeff reached Alex, he searched Alex, going through his backpack until he found the cash.

Then the texts from Alex began:

Alex: Dad just took my money. You gonna pay me back? You owe me.

Me: Your money?? I had that exact amount in my wallet and now it's gone.

Alex: It's mine.

Me: Really? Where did it come from if it is yours?

Alex: So many people owe me money. You are going to give that back to me now!

Alex was enraged by his dad. Jeff was enraged by his son. I was shocked, exhausted, and still loved him.

Later that morning, Jeff and I prayed. I prayed for wisdom, for words, for directions.

"God, you have a plan for this boy. Please keep getting him there. I don't know why we are heading down this all too familiar path again, but what I do know is that you are here in this moment. This did not surprise you, God. I know you have a plan. Now we must continue to wait until it is revealed. Help us to wait. Thank you for being in control of my chaos and for the peace I feel. May Alex awake with a NEW God-inspired, CLEAR direction for his life. Amen."

Chapter Twenty-One

June 15, 2013

I am in an all too familiar place. Feeling like taking a breath is almost too much to bear. The confusion, the pain, the feeling of impending doom surrounds me. How could he go down this path again? How could he be so weak? I fear for what God must do this time.

"Oh, God. I know you love this boy. I know he doesn't deserve your mercy, but he is so in need of it. How will he ever let this go and truly become who you've created him to be? I trust in you, God. I know you have his best interest as your goal."

I read something today that said, "When you can do nothing but pray, that that in and of itself, is an action. It is not doing nothing. It is an ACT of faith. In fact, there is nothing more powerful you can do. Going before the throne of God is a majestic powerful action." I pray, and then I wait for God to do something. It is faith that allows me to do so. So, I wait, trying to pretend what my eyes are seeing isn't happening because my outward actions have so few options.

While I wait, I pray. I pray for Alex to be pierced by God's love and given a desire to follow Him; for Alex to meet God, experience God in a whole new way, a way like never before, for God to intervene and get Alex's attention. Asking God to get Alex's attention is the hardest thing to pray. This is where the most faith comes in because I have to trust that God truly loves Alex enough to heal him. It is scary to think that I am praying for the God of the universe, the God who is all powerful, all present, all knowing, to unleash Himself on Alex. I'm so thankful He is a loving God. I pray for God to get Alex's attention, if at all possible, without the police having to be part of it, while at the same time accepting this may be part of God's plan.

I watch all the other kids his age, and I wonder why he can't be healthy and moving on the right path. Why my son? I've tried so hard to be a good example. I've tried to follow God's teachings. I've tried to be Christ-like. I know the why doesn't really matter, but this time around I'm having a harder time not thinking about it. I look at other people who aren't godly or haven't raised their children in godly homes, and I'm so confused, and at times envious, at how normal these kids are.

"I'm tired God. I'm scared. I'm worn. I'm amazed I have tears left to cry."

Alex rarely comes home. When he does, it might be to take a shower, occasionally mow the lawn, tell me he loves me, then disappear again.

A few days ago, I received a phone call from a friend of his. This friend said Alex was hanging out with Troy again. Troy is making a special kind of crack. The friend thought Alex was using it. Alex has been accused of stealing money from a friend's house, which he denies. He is in deep, and either doesn't know it, or more likely won't admit it. God, we need you!

June 21, 2013

Alex has been gone for two days. He texts me to tell me where he is, but won't come home. He says (or at least tells me) he is with people, names that I do not recognize, but he never tells me where exactly he is.

"God, I don't have a clue what to do. Is there nothing? I know you are in charge. I know you will snatch him back. I know you have a plan. Forgive me for wanting it now. I'm so worn. I'm angry, defeated, confused, and in disbelief that we are here again. I find myself trying not to focus on how unfair I feel this entire situation is. I have been praying for God to not let me be angry or envious. I continue to try to understand how ungodly people who have done obviously sinful things and have exposed their kids to those things, have seemingly normal kids, while I have done everything in my power to follow God and expose my kids to positive, healthy things, and yet my kids are a complete mess. I keep reminding myself that, "You, God, have a plan. You have something amazing to expect my kids to do. Reveal it, God. Please reveal it."

Chapter Twenty-Two

August 2013

To our uttered amazement, Alex returned to school at Greenville College. As we moved him back into his dorm his excitement was palpable. The campus was alive with other students returning. His roommate, James, and his family had arrived at almost the same time as we did. I saw a woman and man standing in the parking lot behind Joy Hall looking like they didn't quite belong. I heard the man speak and immediately knew he had to be James' father. The English accent gave it away. As Jeff introduced himself to James' father, I extended my hand to his mother. I told her I was Alex's mom, and she greeted me with a warm smile.

Jeff, Alex, James, his parents and I walked up four flights of stairs countless times carrying boxes, clothes, school supplies, two mini fridges, a microwave, a TV, an X-Box, LOTS of food, toiletries, and countless other things two young college boys need to clutter their dorm room.

We spent the next hour arranging and putting away. The boys discussed who got which side of the room, and what was the most efficient way to arrange the furniture, so as to have the greatest amount of space: Fridges under the now bunked beds, an area with a rug and a futon for gaming and watching TV, and separate areas for each for studying, food, and clothes.

Alex laughed and joked with other boys from 4th floor Joy, met a few new students, and reconnected with old ones. It seemed to me that he was happy to finally be back to school, happy that things would settle into a routine again. He was looking forward to his independence and planned to get a job to help finance his fun time on campus that semester.

Before the end of that day, Alex had indeed gotten a job. The lady in charge of the dining hall hired him on the spot, once she saw his face and put his name with it.

"You are Alex Davis? If I had remembered your name, I wouldn't have even needed you to come in to meet me."

"I had forgotten how much she loved me," Alex said with a smirk and an audible chuckle when he shared his good news with me.

Things were falling into place. He was settled into his dorm about a week early. He had already snagged a job on campus, and he was excited and energetic about all of it. However, if I had listened to my gut, I would have already seen the anxiety beginning to stalk him, seeping into his pores.

A few weeks passed and Alex was, I thought, attending classes, getting his schedule figured out in his head, and learning how to balance working and studying. Every time we talked on the phone, he was just finishing work or preparing to go to work. It was shortly after the semester got under way that he began sharing with me that he was having trouble sleeping, that he felt very anxious, that he wasn't going to classes, and he didn't know if he could do "this." I encouraged him by telling him how normal it is to feel overwhelmed with being on your own and how everyone has a difficult time transitioning to college and being away from home.

It was just a week or so later that he said he wanted to come home to see his doctor. Alex wanted to change his depression medicine and maybe get on something for anxiety.

Within two days after changing his medication, I began to notice something wasn't right. Alex's speech began to speed up. His thoughts jumped from one topic to the next. He told me that he finally had the energy to do things, but now he had so many ideas in his head that he couldn't make any decisions.

This progressed, and he made several phone calls to me. Most of the time his ideas didn't make complete sense, but he would quickly become angry when I didn't understand or if I asked too many questions. He was demanding. Asking for irrational things... $20,000 to buy a motorcycle or maybe a new Mustang. Furious when I would say no, then saying he was sorry and that he loved me.

It was a Sunday, and I had just arrived home from singing at church all morning. I was sitting in my little red convertible in the garage when my phone rang. It was Alex.

"I wanted to let you know, I'm going away for a little while. Don't be worried. I met a man in the forest, and he is going to show me the way. I won't be able to talk to you, but don't be worried. I'm going to turn my phone off, but don't be worried. I'm just going to go away for a while."

Flashes of another voice from many years before flitted into my mind. I panicked.

"What do you mean you are going away? Where? Who is this person you are talking about? You are scaring me, Alex. I don't want you to go. Who is this person?"

"You don't need to be scared. The man in the forest is going to show me the way. He is going to lead me to where I have always been. I am going to turn my phone off now. Don't be worried."

"Alex, this doesn't make sense. I think you need help. I love you. Please don't turn your phone off."

"He knows things. He is going to share them with me. He is going to take me where I need to be. I am going away. Don't be worried. I love you."

"Alex, please DON'T TURN YOUR PHONE…."

My heart is thumping in my throat, I can feel a panic spreading through my chest.

"What do I do? Oh God! What do I do?"

"FATHER IN HEAVEN I NEED YOU NOW!!!" I yell at the top of my voice. "Holy Spirit, you need to be with Alex right now. I cannot be there to protect him, but YOU can! Help me, Father. Help me! I don't know how to"…my phone barely gets half a ring out before I punch the home button. It is a number I do not recognize, a voice I do not know. The man from the forest?

"Hi, ummm, I am a friend of your son's. I ummm, I'm really worried about him. He has been acting really strangely for a couple of weeks now, and, ummmm, I've been trying to keep an eye on him, so he can be safe, but I just don't think I can anymore. I ummm think he needs to go to the hospital, and I wanted to ask if you were ok if I took him there?"

Holy Spirit, you sent me an answer!

"I'm terrified for him right now. He just told me that he was going away for awhile with the man from the forest. He kept repeating things that didn't make sense. I'm scared he is going to hurt himself. I doubt he will go with you to the hospital, but if you can get him to go, PLEASE take him. Do you know where he is? How will you find him?"

"I have a good idea where he may be. I'll go there first."

Before I hang up, I make this friend promise to call me when he finds Alex.

I call Jeff to tell him something is very wrong with Alex. He is really sick, we need to be ready to go to Greenville.

Within 20 minutes, my phone rings again. Alex and the friend are on their way to

Greenville Regional Hospital. Jeff and I are on the highway in 10 minutes.

My mind is swirling. "Is it drugs? Something else?"

"God, we need you."

I make the necessary phone calls as Jeff drives. I pray and sing and pray and sing as a sickening feeling of impending doom surrounds me.

Alex's friend greets us as we enter the hospital. I hug this young man I have never met before, and tell him how grateful we are for his calling us and getting Alex to the hospital.

Alex is sitting in a hospital bed chatting away with the doctor who is in the room. He isn't making much sense.

"Hi! Why are you guys here? I told the doctor if he would just let me explain, it would all make sense. I'm looking for answers. I'm really fine. You guys can just go home."

In the hallway, the doctor explains that Alex's tox screen has come back clean, no drugs in his system.

"Your son needs to receive treatment, and he needs to be hospitalized, but our hospital does not have a psychiatric department. We need to move him to another hospital that can give him the care he needs. Where would you like me to try? Around here or closer to your home?"

"In Springfield, if possible," I reply.

"OK. I'll have the nurses start making phone calls to see who can take him."

This is new territory. Alex is clearly not making sense. Talking in circles, but very positive and upbeat. I silently pray as he chatters away.

After more than an hour, Jeff and I are informed that there are no hospitals that are either willing to take him as a transfer patient or that have beds available.

"What are our options?"

"We cannot keep him here."

Dr. Apple! She will know what to do. She answers after a couple of rings. This doctor has meant the world to me. She has been so much more than a doctor. She has allowed me to be a partner in the care my children have received. She has made me feel valuable, knowledgeable, and a key component to the solution over and over and over. She made herself available to me through her home number. I have often wondered if I received special treatment, or if she did this with many patients. Either way, I honored this offering by never taking advantage, although, I have had to call on several occasions in moments of crisis.

It is she that I turn to once again. I quickly explain what has transpired in the last several weeks and more specifically the last few hours. I tell her that the doctor thinks he should be admitted for treatment, but the hospital cannot find anyone who will take him as a transfer. I explain to her that I don't know what to do.

In the end, her advice is to have Alex discharged from the hospital in Greenville to Jeff and me, and we are to drive him directly to Memorial Hospital, so that they can evaluate him and admit.

The doctors at Greenville Regional Hospital advise us not to stop anywhere, not for gas, not for food, but to drive directly to Memorial. They are fearful Alex may try to make a run for it. Because of this, I ride in the back seat with him, that familiar feeling of doom welling up inside of me, as I silently pray and sing.

The trip to Memorial does not go as planned. After hours of waiting, the doctor's evaluation does not require hospitalization. Instead, we are told to take him home, make an appointment with a psychiatrist, and not let him out of our sight.

"Do you have any questions?"

"What are we supposed to do? He needs help. I'm not comfortable taking him home."

"Oh, would you like the doctors to come back and re-evaluate? Mr. Davis, is that what YOU would like or would you rather go home?"

"I'd rather go home ma'am," Alex says as he flashes a smile that could melt your heart.

"Of course, he would rather go home. What am I supposed to do? How do I keep him safe?" I am barely able to say without crying

"I suggest you not let him out of your sight."

Stunned, I cannot believe what I am hearing, but the emotional and physical exhaustion is just too much, and I begin to cry. But it doesn't help.

We drive home. Alex's nonsensical chatter continues. I pray, cry, and sing.

When we arrive home, it is about 1 a.m. My eyes sting with exhaustion, but my adrenaline pushes me on. I quickly wash my face, brush my teeth, and gather a few blankets and a pillow, so I can sleep on Alex's bedroom floor. He will not hurt himself on my watch. I will watch over,

142

protect, and fight for this baby of mine until I can no longer breathe.

Alex protests my sleeping on his floor, but gives up the fight once he sees how determined I am.

As he lay in his bed, I am transported to a much sweeter time when I would watch him sleep. I could watch him for hours when he was an infant. I remember hearing his little body shift and flip and turn until his breathing became even and his body became still and sleep overcame him. But tonight, sleep would not come.

Chapter Twenty-Three

I awaken to Alex squatting beside me. He is whispering to me that he is going for a walk and not to worry because he will signal for me if he needs me. I jolt awake as I realize that I must have fallen asleep and that he is trying to climb out his egress bedroom window. I manage to talk him out of this, but I lose the fight when he walks out of his room and up the stairs and on to the back deck.

As he looks up at the star splattered sky, he forcefully claims, "Can't you see they are signaling? They are watching, you know. You understand what I am saying, right? The signs are all around us, if you just look. You understand the signs. Am I making sense?"

"No, sweetheart. You aren't."

More forcefully, "They are there if you just look! The black and the meaning; it is all there. How can you not understand?"

"Sweetheart, I think you are sick."

Almost violent, "You aren't hearing what I am saying! How can they understand? It is a

sign you know? They are all around us if you will
just see. Does that make sense?

"Can we go back into the house? Are you
hungry? I'm hungry. Let's get something to
eat."

At this, he brushes through the patio
door and sits at the kitchen table. I pull snacks
out and set them before Alex. He begins picking
up packages and reading the labels or the words
on the box.

"Distilled....distilled there is a message
there. I think they are trying to tell me
something. Division. What do you think that
means? I think they are signaling to me."

On and on it went.

For the next 10 days, Jeff and I would take turns staying with Alex. We did what the doctors said and never left him alone. Most of this time, he was confused, paranoid, not making sense, and his irritability would erupt into explosive anger. The sweet, generous, kind-hearted boy I know had disappeared, and in his place was this person who had hijacked my Alex.

"Father in Heaven, we need you here. We need your wisdom. Please help us."

Alex's confusion and suspicions were intensified when we would leave the house. He would see cars with government license plates and be completely convinced that we were being followed. He was certain that the President of the United States was trying to kill him. If someone had a cell phone peeking out of his or her pocket, Alex believed that person was recording him. He would forcibly insist that I turn off my phone and stop recording. His anxiety would become so visible, it was painfully uncomfortable to watch.

It took a type of constant awareness, which I had never before had to offer, for every moment he was in our presence. It was utterly exhausting, extremely frightening, and created an anxiety in me that felt as if an engine were in my chest. I could feel the cogs and wheels whirling and my heart pound in the background every single waking moment.

When I was with Alex, it was an intense feeling of responsibility. I didn't want to cause any additional anxiety to him, but what caused him increased anxiety was so random; it was like walking in a hidden minefield. I never knew what would set him off. He would get angry if I didn't understand his cryptic speech, furious if I didn't agree with his outlandish ideas, and irate if he thought I was trying to control him in any way. I was also on constant suicide watch, fearing that he would steal away to hurt himself if I turned my back or took a shower or did anything other than have my eyes constantly on him. It was a miserably, terrifying all-encompassing feeling.

When I wasn't with him, I was either at work or supposed to be sleeping, but my hyper-awareness, responsible self would not let my mind stop focusing on if he was safe, if he was peaceful or angry, or if he had finally fallen asleep.

As Jeff's and my exhaustion increased, Alex's ability to sleep decreased. This was my first experience with a psychotic episode, but I would learn that the longer the event lasted, the harder it is for the body to sleep. The longer the person doesn't sleep, the more intense the psychotic episode will become, and round and round it goes. By the time this episode was over, Alex had not slept, for even a few minutes, in over 12 days.

Those moments when I was alone were my refuge. I would run to the throne of God and weep at His feet. I have never in my life prayed more than I prayed then. I was in constant communication with God. I would begin my day crying out to God in prayer and praising him in song as I drove to work. I would be wrecked emotionally, physically exhausted, but I would call out to my Savior with every fiber of my being as I sobbed at His feet.

I would cry out.

"I know he belongs to you, Father. I know you will heal him. I know you love him. Show me what to do, Father. Give me wisdom. I'll do whatever you want me to do."

This was familiar behavior by now. I had cried out to my Abba so many times before. He had the answer. I knew Alex would be OK. I didn't know when it would happen, but I knew with a certainty like I had never known before that he WOULD BE OK. I just had to wait for whenever that would be.

"Father, help me to hold on to you. I know you are in control. I do not understand this, but I KNOW you are the one in control. Oh, Father in Heaven, save my son."

The day finally came for Alex to see Dr. Hardwick. I was afraid he would not be willing to go to the doctor, so Jeff went with us to ensure Alex's physical arrival. We left the office with several prescriptions. Two that would begin to get the psychotic behavior and thoughts under control, one that would decrease his anxiety, and one that would make him sleep. Dr. Hardwick explained how important it was for him to sleep. Without sleep, he would become well.

Alex was adamantly against the medications, which his father and I found ironically hypocritical, considering all the substances that he had willingly dumped into his body. He was insistent that there were horrible side effects and that he wasn't able to control this drug like he could the ones he chose to ingest, that this was all part of the plot to kill him and control him. It was no small miracle when he decided he would take the medicine. It was just another miracle in a season of miracles.

The first night he took the medication, I had hoped for complete and utter rest for our home, but it was not to be. Although he was able to rest, for the first time in almost 14 days, it wasn't peaceful, and it wasn't quality. The next few nights were continued battles and anxious moments when he would refuse the medication, and I would pray that he would take the medication as if our lives depended on it, because they did.

One day of meds turned into two into five into seven, and I began to see glimpses of my Alex. His smile was intermittently returning. His sweet thoughtful nature would slip through a dark explosive moment.

After two weeks the balance had shifted, and I was seeing Alex more and more. His anxiety was slipping away. His words were making sense, and his anger was more tempered. He was attending regular visits with his doctor; medications were adjusted, issues were half-heartedly discussed. He admitted to a lot of drug use, and the doctor explained how this was exacerbating the psychosis. The key to his recovery was to stop using street drugs, so he did.

I was beginning to breathe again. Alex's anxiety was still an issue, but most of the darkness associated with it was falling away. He was sweet, thoughtful Alex again, at least most of the time. I was praising God for the miracle of medicine and for insurance that provided a good doctor and medication we could afford. Most of all, I was thankful that Alex was staying off the street drugs and actually taking his medication.

Before some of my prayers could even reach the Heavens, the familiar feeling of impending doom began to, once again, permeate my entire body. There was no big moment. No specific event that brought it, but it was as if the winds of Alex's mood had shifted, and I caught the scent in the air. Flashes of anger, moments of confused, mixed words were forcibly spoken. We were heading back to a place I dreaded. Was he not taking his meds? Was he using again? Questions I feared to know the answers to flooded my mind. How can we be doing this again?

"Father in Heaven, please help my son. Please show him how to make wise decisions. Keep him from drugs, and make him take those medications."

I would have long, drawn out discussions with Alex about how important the medications were, how he needed to stay clean, how I was seeing him slip back to a dark place, and it was scaring me.

"God loves you and has a better plan for you. I don't know what it is, but he has something amazing planned for you, but you have to get well first."

Several times I convinced him to get back onto the meds, and again, I would see him brighten, only to notice those dark spots popping up again.

Christmas 2013 came and went rather uneventfully, and I did not ignore the value in this. Uneventful was a complete and awesome gift from God. Alex was home. We were a family. There was a tentative peace, a constant waiting for the other shoe to drop, but at least in that moment the shoes were all neatly placed by our front door, and it gave me a string to hold onto.

As 2014 got under way, life continued with a certain level of familiarity. In the next several months, Alex would hold several different jobs. He was hanging with the wrong crowd again, and all my begging, reasoning, and praying were not making the immediate change I had hoped for. But none-the-less, life still had a tentative sense of calm, and I hoped that Alex was making the right choices in spite of his friends.

But the flashes of anger were becoming more frequent; his presence at home was less and less, and it was evident that he was back to all the same behaviors that got him to the psychotic event we had experienced about six months before. Impending doom had found me again.

Chapter Twenty-Four

Mothers' Day 2014 was an exceptionally difficult day. Alex was nowhere in sight. He had been MIA for several days. He promised to be home at some point, but lunch was over and gifts had already been exchanged, and there was no word from him.

As we sat around the dining room table talking, I received a text message from our 17-year-old son Andrew. He was in his room just upstairs and the text irritated me. Why did he find it necessary to text me when he is just a floor above me?

> I need to talk to you. Can you please come upstairs?

Something in my heart dropped. I had noticed his mood was dipping, his irritability was elevated, and the time he spent alone in his room had increased. For the past several weeks, his doctor had been titrating him from a medication he had been taking for his bipolar disorder for years. The plan was to get off this medication and begin a new one, but as the level of medication in his system was declining, so was his mood.

When I walked into his room, he was lying on his bed.

"I need help. I need you to take me to the hospital."

"What is going on?"

"I'm afraid I'm going to hurt myself. I need to go to the hospital."

The whirling of my insides immediately swung into high gear. How could I have missed how low he was? How could I have been so wrapped up in Alex that I missed it?

"Father forgive me. Help me to get the right help for Drew. Give the doctors wisdom to know what to do."

I quickly found Jeff and told him we needed to leave now to take Drew to the emergency room. I apologized to my family, who had joined us for dinner, and told them quickly what was happening. We were in the car in less than 10 minutes. That familiar impending doom was threatening to swallow me up.

As the hours ticked by, the assessment was done, and it was clear that Drew needed to be admitted, but the hospital was having a difficult time finding a facility that had an open bed for Drew. Fearing he would harm himself, the doctor decided that Drew would be kept in the ER until arrangements could be made. I decided immediately to stay with him. He was scared, and I was quickly noticing terrifyingly familiar behaviors, as he was in the early stages of his first full-blown psychotic episode. There would be no releasing of Drew for quite some time.

After almost 24 hours, we were notified that there was a bed available at Lincoln Prairie Behavioral Center. Due to the threat of harm to himself, the hospital would not allow me to drive him there. Instead, Drew was taken by ambulance, as I closely followed behind in our car.

Lincoln Prairie quickly admitted him, whisked him up in an elevator, and began to get him into a room. By now the psychotic episode was full blown. He was screaming, terrified, refusing medication, begging me to take him home, swearing if I didn't take him home, he'd kill himself. Not exactly the argument to use to get yourself out of a mental facility. It was almost more than I could bear.

He is screaming now. Yelling, being violent, writhing on the floor-totally out of control and out of his mind with sickness.

"YOU ARE HURTING ME! STOP! YOU ARE HURTING ME!! MOM, PLEASE DON'T LET THEM HURT ME. I'M GOING TO KILL YOU. YOU ARE HURTING ME. STAY AWAY FROM ME!"

"Father in Heaven, help my son. Please help him to think clearly. Please, Lord, help him. Give me strength to endure this continued assault on my children. Help me to remember, you are good even when life isn't."

I watch the nurse make a phone call, and within a minute or so huge male orderlies come and hold Andrew down to the ground. He is so small, but his rage, fueled by a betrayal of his own mind, is encompassing him, and the fury is like none I have ever seen from him. He is kicking and screaming as they hold him down and a needle quickly punctures his arm. His screams fill the air.

"EEEEEEE YOU ARE HURTING ME. MOM, DON'T LET THEM HURT ME," he sobs between the fits of rage.

The orderlies back away as the medication they have administered begins to take hold. I creep near him. Needing to comfort him. To hold him in my arms, to tell him I love him, but as I draw near, he begins to scream at me.

"THIS IS YOUR FAULT. I HATE YOU. TAKE ME HOME. MOMMA, PLEASE TAKE ME HOME," he screams and sobs.

I try to hold him, but he recoils.

"GET AWAY FROM ME. THIS IS ALL YOUR FAULT."

I back out of the room. I'm sobbing. Every part of my being is hurting. I watch him writhing on the floor, hiccupping, sobbing, and gasping for air. A nurse puts her hand on my shoulder and walks me to the elevator. As the elevator doors closed, flashes of leaving Alex there three years before are surrounding me.

"How much more can I take, Father?" I said audibly as the tears were overtaking me. "How much more?"

I arrive home by 11:00 p.m. the Monday after Mother's Day, emotionally empty. The anxiety in my chest is high, and it threatens to overtake me. I haven't heard from Alex, but there are half dead flowers and a card that he has left for me.

I sit on the kitchen floor and weep. After I regain my composure, I wash my face, brush my teeth, and go to the kitchen to use the phone on the wall to call and check on Drew. A nurse answers. She tells me he is sleeping soundly, and how sorry she is that I am going through this. She asks how I am, and I don't even know how to respond. This woman could have no idea of the struggle I have had for the last four years. She cannot know that this latest episode is just another in a long string of terrifying events that has to do with mental illness.

As the days pass, Drew is not getting better. In fact, he is getting worse. He is refusing meds, something he has never done before. This is a clear indication as to the level of his sickness. The facility clearly doesn't know how to treat him, and it takes them four days before they realize that I am not a mother who will passively wait for medical professionals to get their acts together.

It is about this time that I find out that the "doctor" who is in charge of Andrew's treatment is not a medical doctor, but instead holds a PhD in psychology. I am furious and demand that an actual medical doctor, one whom is a board-certified pediatric psychiatrist, oversee his care. I am met with much resistance, but I continue to vehemently insist.

After the second day of Drew's digression, I am on the phone calling everyone I can get a number for asking, no begging, for help. Telling anyone who will listen that Drew isn't like most of the kids they get at Lincoln Prairie. He isn't there because of choices he has made. He is there because he got a crappy deal when it comes to genetics. He is suffering from a full-blown psychotic episode that was brought on by the change in his medication, and he needs a board-certified psychiatrist to oversee his care.

I do research myself, and talk to Dr. Apple, and we decide that the best thing to do is to put Drew back on the medication he was on before. The problem is that Dr. Apple does not have privileges at this facility, which means she can do nothing. I again make phone calls and even personally confront this "doctor" who is caring for Drew. I make it VERY clear what probably needs to be done to help Drew to get out of the psychotic episode. He needs to be put back on the medication he was on before, and this needs to happen now.

After almost 10 days of watching Drew get worse because he is not receiving the correct treatment, and through a barrage of my constant phone calls, complaints, and insistence, an actual psychiatrist decides that she will oversee Drew's care, and they begin to administer the old medication. Within a few days, we see drastic improvement, and our Drew begins to peek through the darkness.

As Drew continues to slowly improve, Alex is quickly declining. He is almost never home anymore. He disappears for multiple days at a time. When he does show up, he is angry, irritable, and secretive.

Chapter Twenty-Five

One Sunday, before we leave for church, Jeff needs to move Alex's car. After Jeff moves the car and for whatever reason, opens Alex's glove box, he finds several bags of marijuana and a variety of drug paraphernalia. The dread in my chest rises, pushes, and completely encompasses me.

Jeff and I drive to church in complete silence, both afraid to begin the conversation that will be exhausting. We both know that something must be done, but I am terrified of what that something may be.

"Father in Heaven, how much more? Holy Spirit, we need you. We need your wisdom, your presence. Your answer to this will be good. I know this, Father. Please give me the ability to do whatever it is you will ask of me."

On the way home from church, it is Jeff who speaks.

"He cannot live in our house and have drugs."

My heart drops to the bottom of my chest like a boulder being dropped into a river.

"I know," I whisper, the tears already overwhelming me. Everything in me wants to scream. A panic is smothering me. I feel as if a weight is crushing my chest, and I'm having a hard time making my lungs work. I want to fight this decision with every fiber of my being, but Jeff is right. Alex cannot bring drugs into our house.

Before we make it home, Jeff and I go to Lincoln Prairie to visit Drew. He is doing much better. He is getting back to his normal self again. We sit and talk in the visitors' room. We play some games, dribble a basketball a little, and visit. There is no mention of Alex. Drew's emotional balance is too delicate. I'm trying to focus on Drew. Attempting to live in the moment, but the feeling of impending doom is welling up inside me, thinking of the confrontation that is about to take place at home.

It is decided that Alex will be given a choice. We will either call the police, or he will agree to go back into treatment. Both choices make me want to throw up.

Jeff and I enter Alex's room. As he lay there sleeping, a grief was filling my chest. How could this be my sweet Alex? Oh, how I would die myself, if I thought it could save him. As Jeff turned on the overhead bedroom light and switched off the fan, Alex barely stirred.

"Alex, you need to wake up. We have some things to talk about."

Needless to say, Alex did not move quickly, and it was clear he was quite confused with sleep and maybe the party from the night before.

"You need to get up, or I'm about to call the police," Jeff says.

"What??" Alex mumbles.

"You need to get up, or I'm calling the police. I found your stash. "

"What? What are you talking about? That's not mine."

"Cut the crap Alex. You cannot bring drugs into our home. Do you know what could happen to your mom if that was found in our home? She could lose her teacher's certificate?"

Alex is now up and moving around his room; his head still foggy, but he is thinking faster than we realize.

"You need help Alex. You need to get some help. You have two choices right now. You are going to let Mom and me take you somewhere for treatment, or am I calling the police? "

Alex continues to move around his room.

"I need to get some fresh air. I cannot breathe. I f******* cannot breathe."

The gravity of the situation is beginning to take hold, and the tension is building. Jeff is becoming more insistent that Alex make a decision. Alex keeps stating that they aren't even his drugs, and I am failing miserably to make the event as peaceful as possible. The engine in my chest is overwhelming me, whirling, sinking me.

Alex is not making a whole lot of sense; clearly the anxiety of this moment is consuming him. He keeps saying that he doesn't know what we are talking about and that he cannot breathe, but he knows enough to worm his way from his bedroom in the basement to our outside deck on the next floor.

Once outside, he hesitates for a moment-pacing back and forth-and then he dashes off the deck and out of our back fence and runs. My gut is to run after him, to bring him back, to hold him, to make him be OK, but all I'm thinking is that he doesn't even have shoes on his feet.

"He is not welcome here anymore." Jeff's words punch me so hard I feel as if the air has been removed from my lungs, and my heart is going to explode. Feelings of sudden abandonment wash over me and drown me. My mind understands the truth of what Jeff is saying, but my heart cannot accept its reality.

"He has nowhere to go," I breathe.

"He made his choice. We cannot allow him to stay here and bring drugs into our house."

"What is he going to do? He has nothing. He isn't going to stay away. He will come back."

"He is not welcome here anymore. You need to pack his things and put them on the front porch."

I cannot even use my words as I am engulfed in a despair that chokes my ability to think. Sobbing, I find myself in his bedroom, with an empty suitcase. I lie on the floor and weep, taking huge gulps of air, reminding myself to breathe in and out. For the first time in the last four years, I want to just curl into a ball and never come back out.

Tears have blurred my vision. There is an enormous weight on my chest. It is a physical pain, palpable. I think I'm going to throw up, but there is a task at hand, so I quickly try to pack what I think Alex will need. Warm things. I don't want him to get cold. His favorite boots.

Clean underwear. His toothbrush. I stuff anything that may protect him into the case. I cannot believe I am packing my son's things because he is no longer welcome in my home. The sobs overwhelm me again, and I fall on the floor.

"Holy Spirit, I need you now. Help us, Father. Help us."

Friends and family begin to show up to comfort us, pray with us. It is as if we are mourning the death of our family. I am now lying on my kitchen floor sobbing. People are around me. Praying with me. It feels as if death is engulfing me, as if someone has put an enormous weight inside my chest on top of my heart. I must remind myself to breathe in and out over and over because it seems that I can no longer do this from memory. I have never felt such despair, panic, and separation as I feel in this moment. I'm not even able to pray. I simply say, "Holy Spirit, I need you" over and over and over. There are no other words that come.

Chapter Twenty-Six

Alex is trying to come through the kitchen door, but it is locked. I hear him curse and walk out of the garage and can see him standing outside the front door. I hear him chuckle somewhat when he sees his things packed by the front door. He texts my phone:

Uh, can you let me in?

I freeze. Everything in me wants to throw the door open wide and have my lungs work on their own again, but Jeff's words echoing in my brain stop me. *He isn't welcome here anymore.*

It isn't the first moment when I felt as if I had to choose sides. How do I leave him standing out there? Abandoned. Something I never wanted my babies to EVER experience, but the truth in Jeff's words pulls me back again

"Father, show me how to trust Jeff's lead in this. You know I am weak when it comes to my boys. I want what will make Alex whole again. Help me to follow and trust Jeff's lead."

I ask the Holy Spirit to be with me, and I open the front door.

"Why are my things on the front porch?" Alex asks.

"We told you; you had to get treatment. You cannot live here and bring drugs into our home."

"I need those things Dad took back. They didn't belong to me. I need them back."

"You will have to talk to Dad about that."

Alex is agitated, angry, visibly stressed. He asks if he can come in and get some of his things. He says he needs the keys to his motorcycle. I tell him he will have to talk to his dad, and he doesn't push this issue.

He packs his computer, even though I strongly urge him not to take it. He has hawked so many things to buy drugs. I fear that is where his MacBook Air will end up, and I remember when we gave it to him before he left for Greenville College. It felt like a lifetime away.

I am sobbing as I watch him go through his things. He opens the bag I have packed and pulls out some of the items and questions some of the other ones.

"You are really kicking me out, huh?" He says this so I can hear but with a smirk that shows defiance.

"Don't worry about me. I'll be fine."

"Alex, you need help. I'm so scared. "

He hugs me, tells me he loves me, zips up his bag, and walks up the stairs and out the front door taking pieces of me with him.

A couple of nights later, Alex shows up at my front door. He begs to come in, saying he needs something from his room. It is clear that he is extremely confused, and his thoughts are jumbled. He is in the kitchen pacing.

"Can you hear that? Do you hear that?" He says; his eyes are filled with terror. "I never should have come here because the demons have followed me, and now they are in our house."

My heart is moving faster than I think it is possible; my fear is growing. I am no stranger to demons.

Chapter Twenty-Seven

I am nine years old. It is dark in the room I share with my older sister. So, when I open my eyes, it takes a minute for them to focus. I can see something seated in a chair that is placed at the foot of my bed. My sister and I had received director's chairs for Christmas. Mine was aqua-green; her's banana yellow. Our respective chairs had each of our names in crisp white block lettering across the top, just like all the famous movie directors. I so wanted to be famous when I was little. This gift was a nod to that dream.

I blinked my eyes, sure that I was either imagining something or misinterpreting shadows, making them into something that is really nothing, like many nine-year-old girls can do in the middle of the night. But as I blinked and blinked and blinked the figure did not disappear. I slowly sat up in bed continuing to blink my eyes. What was I seeing, and why was it sitting in my chair? As I sat up, the figure rose as one standing up from a chair would. I saw its back raise up, and then the figure turned to face me. It was a face with no features, hollow. I knew where its eyes should be, but there were no eyes; I knew where its mouth should be, but there was no mouth, and I knew where its nose should be, but only gaping holes were in those places. It was not flesh; it was spirit-like. It had definite shape, but the lines were blurred.

As I watched it rise up and turn toward me, it began to speak. After all these years, I do not remember exactly what words it spoke, but I remember the message clearly. This spirit told me my dad was coming back for me, that I was to go on a specific date, at a specific time, to a specific place, and my dad would be waiting for me. I was instructed to be there, so that my dad could come take me with him.

I wasn't scared for one moment. I was ecstatic! How could this be happening? How could Daddy be coming back? Oh, how I had missed him! I couldn't wait to see him! I jumped out of bed and ran through our dark house and woke up my mother. I told her about my messenger with an excitement that I'm sure was too high for the middle of the night, but it isn't often that someone's dad comes back from the dead to get them! And I only had a few days to wait! My heart was racing with a happiness that I thought had been lost forever.

But confusion set in as my mother scrambled to her feet and fumbled as she turned on the lamp beside her bed and told me to tell her again what had just happened, so I did. But her face wasn't reflecting the joy in mine. She went white as a terror seemed to creep into her chest.

The next thing I remember was my mother walking from room to room praying and calling out, "In the Name of Jesus be gone! You have no place here. This child, this house, belongs to Jesus! In the Name of Jesus be gone! You have no place here." I wasn't the least bit scared as I crawled back into bed. All I wanted to do was have time pass quickly, so the day would get here, and I could see my daddy again.

The day FINALLY came. I had a hard time sleeping and couldn't wait until it was time to get up. Today was the day; my dad was coming back for me today! My excitement quickly turned to panic as my mother put me in her car and drove me to my grandparents' house, which was far from where I was supposed to go to meet Dad. I was furious! I couldn't believe she would do this to me. How could she? I had missed him so much. I HAD to get there. I would run. No one would be able to stop me.

My mom put my Uncle Bill, the one who was with us the night Dad died, in charge of me that day. I wasn't even allowed to go to the bathroom with the door closed because it would have been easy to get out of the window and run.

I can remember him trying to talk to me all day, trying to get me interested in something else, trying to distract me as you would a two-year-old who wants the toy someone else is playing with. But all I could do was beg for him to take me to where I was supposed to be.

"I have to meet someone today. Please, please just take me there. Please, I've missed him so much, he wants me to be there! I have to be there! Why won't you take me there? Please....please...please," I sobbed. He tried to hold me, but I was so angry and hurt. I had come so close. How could I lose him again?

Never once did it cross my mind that something was happening that was bigger than I; that I would be walking into something I had no idea how to control if I followed the directions given to me by this spirit. Never once did I think about my safety. Never once did I consider that the tracks where I was to meet Dad was the planned location of the second attempt on my life by this same demon. Never once did it cross my mind that everyone around me was scared to death. Never once did I consider that this would be the second time my mother would have to save my life.

As years passed, this event no longer invoked joy. After I missed my rendezvous point, *a dark, heavy, terrifying presence overcame me every time I thought of this encounter. In fact, to this day, if I would allow it, simply thinking about this experience would cause me to feel enveloped by evil.*

I am jolted back to my present moment.

"They have been telling me to kill myself all day. I'm trying to fight them off, Momma."

My silent prayers are now audible.

"Father in Heaven, we need your spirit here NOW! Send warring angels to surround and protect Alex. Be with him, Father! Calm his mind, protect his body, help him to want to get help."

Alex allows me to pray, but he doesn't stay still long. His cryptic speech is in full force again.

"You know the signs are all around. If you just look for them, you can see them. You know what I mean?"

"Father in Heaven, we need you."

"I'm not going to let him get me, Momma. I know he wants to kill me, but I'm trying really hard to tell him no."

"Alex, you need help, honey."

"The signs are everywhere. I never should have come here. Now the demons are in your house. I have to leave. I have to take them away."

"Alex, please. I want to help you get well. I'm so scared right now," I cry as he is closing the front door behind him.

I fall in a heap on the floor. It is about 1 a.m. I am all alone, as I weep with a force that once again, should empty me, but there is something deep inside me that is clinging to hope.

"Unless the Lord had given me help, I would soon have dwelt in the silence of death. When I said, "My foot is slipping," your love, O Lord, supported me. When anxiety was great within me, your consolations brought joy to my soul." --Psalm 94:17-19

Chapter Twenty-Eight

During this time, we have an army of people praying for and with us. One evening our friends Don and Jennifer meet to pray with just Jeff and me. They bring oil, which we pray over, asking the Holy Spirit to anoint it. We then discuss the idea of anointing our home with this oil, especially in Alex and Drew's rooms. So, we do.

All four of us go into Drew's room and pray. As we pray, Jeff draws a cross in oil on the doorway and above his bed. We pray for healing and for peace for Drew. We move to Alex's room and again pray. We pray for protection for our family, for warring angels to surround us and stand guard, to bring peace, to fight off the demons that are surely trying to take our family down. Reminding these spirits that they are forgetting that Alex and Drew belong to the God of the Universe, and there is NOTHING that can be done to change that! Jeff draws a cross directly above Alex's bed, beside his window, and outside the doorway to his room. (In fact, these crosses can still be seen there as I am writing this.)

Another night we meet in our home, gathered around our dining room table that dates back over 100 years. I stop to wonder what other tragedies this table may have witnessed, as 10 prayer warriors sit around it, holding hands, lifting my family, my Alex, up in prayer.

Before the prayer even begins, I am overwhelmed with grief. There is a heaviness that encompasses me, even while a hope fills me up. I KNOW GOD WILL bring my boy back. I KNOW IT!

"Father, let Alex accept the help he needs. Let him want to come home. Let him come home and feel so much peace here that he will want to stay," prays our friend Don.

For the next nine days, Alex spirals into another full flown psychotic event. He calls yelling and screaming for me to give him his motorcycle key. Using everything he can think of to guilt me into giving it to him. There is no question about whether his dad or I will give him the key, as doing so is surely the same as handing him a gun. But the guilt of abandoning Alex is overwhelming me. I have no idea where he is staying. Is he is in someone's home, the back seat of a car, or sleeping in an alley?

"I cannot get to work without my bike. I'm going to starve to death. Don't you care about me? I f****** need my motorcycle key. You need to give me those drugs back. The people they belong to are threatening to kill Dad if he doesn't give them back."

"Dad has destroyed everything, Alex."

"Then he needs to pay for it all. I don't have a way to pay for it. They are going to kill Dad."

Fear for our safety is growing. It grows so much that Jeff pulls one of his handguns out and lays it in clear sight on his dresser. He shows me where the key to the safety is hidden and how quickly it can be removed. I am shaking during this show and tell. The sight of the gun makes me sick to my stomach.

Scenarios run through my head. What if someone breaks in and tries to hurt us while we are sleeping? What if Jeff isn't home, and it is just me? What if Alex manages to get in, and Jeff mistakes him for someone else?

"Father, help us."

December 1977 flashes through my soul. How can this be where we are?

The anxiety causes neither Jeff nor me to be able to sleep very soundly. Every creak causes both of us to be on alert. Sometimes Alex calls in the middle of the night to yell at me. Sometimes he calls to beg for the key to the motorcycle. Sometimes he calls to talk about things that make no sense. I always answer; afraid that this could be the last call he will ever make, knowing I could never forgive myself or remember how to make my lungs work again if this were to happen.

And then one night, at about 10 p.m. Alex texts me:

```
I'm coming home to talk to Dad
about my motorcycle.
```

I panic and show the text to Jeff.

"Tell him, it is too late to come over. We are about to go to bed."

I text this, but within a few minutes, there is a truck in my driveway. I can tell the truck is full of people. We don't know if this truck is full of the people Alex has been talking about, but the possibility makes Jeff very nervous. He calls the police and tells them that our son is acting strange and that we need an officer to come to our home.

A door opens and Alex gets out of the truck, and within moments, the truck backs out of our driveway.

Knowing that if I see Alex, I will melt, I run up the stairs and stand in the hallway, being

180

sure that Alex cannot see me when Jeff opens the door. I can hear Alex asking where I am.

"Where is Mom?"

"She's upstairs. She'll be down in a minute."

I can hear their voices through the walls. I want to warn Alex to run, to leave before the police get there, but my mind knows it is not the right decision.

"Holy Spirit, we need you now."

I take a deep breath and walk down the steps and out our front door and find Alex and Jeff talking. Alex is upbeat and talking about things that don't make sense. I'm not sure at this point how much of it is the drugs and how much is a mental illness.

As he is talking to us, he pulls out a small black wallet size pouch and pulls out a vape and fills it with oil. He tells us he has to use it to help with his anxiety. He doesn't know we have called the police. I want to grab it and throw it in the bushes, but instead I try to sneak it away from him to hide it.

"What are you doing?"

"I think you need to put this away, Alex. I don't want you to get into trouble."

"What are you talking about?"

At that moment, a police car pulls up, and Alex looks at me and laughs.

"You guys called the police?"

"You need help, Alex."

Jeff tries to talk to the officer privately to explain what is going on, that Alex needs help. The officer steps over to speak to Alex and notices Alex's black pouch. He picks it up.

"Whose is this?"

"Mine," Alex replies. It is just some oil I use to calm down.

The officer takes the pouch, opens it and inspects it.

As the officer talks to Alex, it is clear that something is very wrong with Alex, but again it isn't clear if it is drugs or if it is a mental issue. Alex chats away with the officer. Most of what he says doesn't make sense.

I try to explain what is going on with Alex. That he is very sick and needs help. I mention that a friend, who is an officer, had said that if Alex gets arrested, a judge could mandate he go to treatment. The officer listens and agrees that it is possible.

The next thing I know, the officer tells Alex he is under arrest for possession of an illegal substance, handcuffs him, and walks him to the police car. It takes everything in me not to run after them.

How can this be the right decision? Is this really our best option?

"They aren't really arresting me. They aren't going to keep me," Alex is saying as he is looking over his shoulder. I can also hear him tell the officer, "I'm a really big Christian. Just ask my parents. I'm a really big Christian."

I find hope. In this moment of confusion and discombobulation, Alex is claiming Christ! I know he isn't in his right mind, and most of what he is saying has not made any sense, but in that moment, something in him knows where his foundation lies.

Although I know Alex is safe for the moment, I cannot stop my mind from racing. Did we do the right thing in calling the police? What other options did we have? How soon will he see a judge? Will the judge actually require Alex to get help? Will he get into a hospital quickly and get well?

"Father in Heaven, we need you here. Holy Spirit, be with Alex, be with Jeff and me, be in the house." Emotional and physical exhaustion overwhelm me as I pray myself to sleep.

Chapter Twenty-Nine

The screen tells me Alex is calling, and my mind snaps to full attention. I pick it up, and tell Jeff, it's Alex.

"Don't answer it," he says.

"We have to answer it! You have to talk to him. I cannot tell him I won't rescue him."

"Hello?" I listen as Jeff answers.

I can hear Alex say, "Where's Mom?"

"She is sleeping."

"Can you guys please come bail me out since you had me arrested?"

"No, buddy. We aren't going to bail you out."

"Seriously? You won't come get me? What kind of parents are you? You know what kind of people are here? There are demons here, and they are everywhere."

"Alex, you need help. We are hoping you will go before a judge, and he will be able to get you some help."

He laughs, exhales, and I can imagine just how he is holding his head.

"You have no idea what you have done. You have really messed up now. You have no idea what you have done to me."

"You need help, Alex," and Jeff disconnects the call.

My mind is racing, trying to find the words to say, but all I can do is sob.

Time passes. I don't know how much, but the blaring of the phone startles me awake. As I reach to silence it, I look at the clock; it's a little after 1:00 a.m. I have no idea who is calling, as I do not recognize the number. In a panic, I answer.

"Hi, umm my name is Nancy. I am Wayne's mom. Sorry to call you so late, but ummm, I have been receiving some weird voice messages from Alex. He is saying a lot of things that don't make sense. He's been talking about demons all day. He says he is in jail, and he has bailed himself out, but needs someone to come get him. I can't go get him. I just felt I needed to call you."

He bailed *himself* out? I climb out of bed and stand in the darkness of my bathroom, trying not to wake Jeff. I thank her and give her a quick run-down of the most recent events.

"I knew he was having some issues, but I had no idea it was so bad."

My mind is racing again. Where is he? Where will he go? How will the judge mandate he get help now? He is so sick.

"Father, be with Alex. I have no idea where he is, but I KNOW that you know exactly where he is at this very moment. Protect him, Father, and get him the help he needs. "

Somewhere in the midst of all this, I remember that I have to go to work in a few hours and that Drew will be released from his three-week stay at the hospital later in the afternoon. I wonder how much longer I can do this.

"How much longer Lord? How much longer? There is no question that you will heal Alex. I know he will be OK. I just don't know when. I have faith in your promises, Lord. I trust your word. You are a good God even when life isn't. I need you to rescue me. I don't know how much longer I can keep it together."

"May the God of hope fill you with all joy and peace as you trust in him, so that you may overflow with hope by the power of the Holy Spirit." –Romans 15:13

That morning I am scurrying around the house getting ready for my day. I have already showered and dressed as I walk around the house opening up the blinds. As I raise the blinds to the deck, I gasp when I see him. Alex is curled up on the glider that sits on our deck, and he is sound asleep. My heart races. Will Jeff call the police? Should I call the police? Should I let him in? I want to throw open the doors and kneel beside him and hold him and make everything ok, but even as this thought passes through my anxiety-filled mind, the sadness of my inability to make everything OK overwhelms me, and I begin to sob. "Father in Heaven, please be here."

I quietly open the door and creep toward Alex, enveloping him with a warm blanket. The rhythmic up and down of his body's breath is the only movement I see. A flash of him as a baby spreads across my memory. My head hurts for my broken heart. I turn and go without making a noise.

As I tell Jeff that Alex is asleep on our deck, we both wonder how in the world he got here? Later that morning, I would receive text messages from our pastor who said Alex had walked from the police station (several miles away) to his house, which is just a few blocks from our house. Alex had knocked on our youth pastor Tom's door at some point after midnight and asked if he could stay there, but because of Alex's recent illegal activities, mentally unable behavior, and fearing for the safety of his own family, our pastor said no.

Unbeknownst to Alex, the pastor watched Alex roam from one house to another. He was pacing back and forth on random people's front porches. Sometimes he would walk up the front steps of a home and sit in a chair for a short period of time only to get up and leave and repeat this behavior at someone else's house. He was lost. He was not able to rationally think. He was at rock bottom.

Somehow in his wandering, he knew to come home.

"What should we do?" I ask Jeff. "Should we let him in?"

"Yes," is his reply.

I walk back to the deck to wake Alex. He practically jumps out of his skin. He seems confused, exhausted, and relieved as I tell him to get up and come sleep in his bed.

And as he settles underneath his covers, a prayer is answered when he whispers "I feel so at peace here."

Chapter Thirty

Jeff has to go out of town for work that morning, which means I will have to pick up Drew from the hospital alone. I am extremely concerned about his coming home to such chaos. Drew's mental state is tremendously better than it was three weeks ago; however, there is no question that his mental balance is still vulnerable.

I am deeply concerned to leave Alex alone in the house. I stand over him before I leave for work and pray that he sleeps all day long. I know from past experience that psychotic episodes make it difficult to sleep, which in turn exacerbates the symptoms, which makes it harder to sleep, and round and round it goes. "Father, please let Alex be enveloped in peace and deep sleep."

Picking up Drew from the hospital proves to be uneventful, which is a really good thing because my entire morning has been consumed with trying to process what had transpired with Alex in the previous 12-18 hours. Sitting in my SUV in front of Lincoln Prairie, I called Dane, my dear friend and prayer warrior Sherrie's husband, a detective in the Springfield Police Department, who knew well our struggle with Alex. As I explained how Alex had been arrested, bailed himself out, and walked home, I lamented how seemingly nothing constructive had transpired. His court date wasn't for weeks. Way too much time would pass before Alex would be called in front of a judge; too much time before he could even potentially be forced into some sort of treatment. I explained how concerned I was for Drew. He would be home and his mental state was very fragile. Alex had been so unpredictable and violent; I was at a total loss and did not know what to do.

Dane discussed his frustration at how the encounter with the officer had gone, and admitted that unfortunately the luck of the draw with which officer responds, plays a larger role than he would like in how situations are handled. The hope was that Alex would have received help that night and not actually been arrested. Under the circumstances, the officer could have taken Alex to a hospital for treatment instead of arresting him.

Dane tells me that if I feel I need to call the police again that I am to use the words "My son is sick, and he needs to be taken to a hospital." He stressed that I needed to be polite but firm in my request. The thought of calling the police again regarding Alex made my stomach churn and my head swirl. It was a good thing I was sitting in the front seat of my SUV, or I might have passed out.

Later that afternoon, Drew and I arrive home. The house is still quiet. As Drew tries to settle into being home, I am doing everything in my power to make the transition quiet and calm, but inside I am holding back the gates, anticipating the coming destruction. I keep praying that when Alex wakes up, he will be at peace. I pray that he will be willing to go to the hospital, that he will not run or fight, but just accept help. I don't have many words left, so mostly I just ask the Holy Spirit to be there, to be present.

Jeff is traveling back from being out of town, so I am in the house alone with the boys. A feeling of nervous anticipation is filling in the cracks of me, as I hear Alex moving around in his basement bathroom. Sounds of a loud crash, things scattering on the floor, and Alex cussing are rising up. I run down the stairs in an attempt to soothe whatever is happening. Hoping to not disturb Drew while attempting to placate Alex. He is furious. Yelling at nothing and everything all at once. The contents of a drawer from one of the bathroom cabinets is strewn on the floor.

I bend over to pick the things up. "No big deal. Sometimes these drawers come out too easily."

"What the F*** are you doing? Don't pick that up!"

"Buddy, please keep your voice down. Your brother just got home from the hospital, and he is trying to sleep."

"What is he doing here? That boy is evil. He needs to be killed."

"Alex! Don't say such a thing!"

"He is evil and Satan is in him. He needs to leave. Either he leaves or I leave."

"Alex, let's just try to calm down." My mind is racing, trying to stall. I am afraid at any moment he will bound up the stairs and put hands on Drew. I am terrified. I know that I cannot stop that physical attack.

"Father, please bring Jeff home now," I silently pray,

I follow Alex out of his bathroom and up the stairs. He is standing at the fridge filling up a glass of water as I hear the garage door lifting, which means Jeff is home. "Thank you, Jesus," I say silently.

"He better not come in here and start on me. I'll break his neck," Alex hisses.

My heart drops to my toes at the thought of the coming confrontation. My pulse is speeding up. "Holy Spirit be here," I repeat in my mind over and over.

"Alex, stop! Your dad loves you."

"I'll kill both of them," he says with a darkness that doesn't belong to him.

In that moment, Jeff opens the kitchen door and pops his head in. "Everything OK in here?" Jeff looks from Alex to me and then closes the door again.

"Yeah, you better run," Alex snarls, a little too loudly. The kitchen door opens back up, as Jeff steps into the kitchen and closes the door behind him.

"What did you say to me?"
Fear engulfs me, as I run from the kitchen and upstairs. My hands are shaking as I dial 911.

"My son needs help! He is sick and he needs to go to the hospital. He needs help now. I need him to go to the hospital. He is threatening to kill his brother and father."

My heart is about to explode with fear. "Holy Spirit be here. Holy Spirit be here. Holy Spirit be here," I repeat in my mind.

"Ma'am, can you tell me your son's name and your address?"

I give him my baby's name. I cannot believe this is where we are right now. How can this be my sweet, sweet Alex?

"Ma'am, we have an ambulance on the way."

I hang up the phone, but I am pacing like a caged animal.

"Holy Spirit be here. Holy Spirit be here. Holy Spirit be here. Holy Spirit be here," is all I can pray. I have no other words. No other requests. I just need protection to pour over my family. I need the Holy Spirit to be in my house like never before.

I can hear Jeff and Alex talking, but I do not go downstairs.

"Holy Spirit be here."

My phone rings, and it is the police dispatcher.

"Mrs. Davis?"

"Yes?"

"I have an officer who is in front of your house; can you please go meet him? He wants to talk to you."

I glance out my bedroom window to see a Springfield Police Car parked on the street. I walk as quietly and quickly as I possibly can down our stairs and out the front door, trying to not alert Alex. I don't want him to bolt again.

As I approach the police car, the officer emerges.

"Mrs. Davis? I'm officer Volllmer. Dane Cookson talked to me about what has been going on with your son. We've been kind of waiting for your call. Tell me what is going on now."

I quickly re-cap the last 24 hours. It is then that I see the ambulance pulling into my driveway. My heart speeds up, and I again worry that Alex will bolt if he sees the police and the ambulance.

"Holy Spirit be here."

The EMTs quickly get out of their vehicle and ask me where Alex is. I tell them that Alex is in the house, but that I'm afraid he will bolt once he sees them, or worse that he will fight. They assure me that they will be able to contain Alex, but that they will do their best to get him to come with them willingly.

Officer Vollmer and I walk in the front door of the house to find Alex sitting on the back deck with Jeff not far off. Officer Vollmer begins to talk to Alex.

"Hey, bud. How's it going? Want to tell me what is going on here?"

"Nothing. I'm fine. I'm guessing my parents called you," Alex responds with all the charm and sincerity that is his true nature. He is calm, collected, and his sweetness is shockingly genuine.

"Why do you think they called us?'

"I'm not really sure, officer. "

"Alex, they are worried about you. "

"I don't know why they are worried about me. I'm fine. I mean I haven't had much sleep, so I'm really tired. Maybe they are worried about that?"

At that, the paramedics come around the corner. There are two of them. They are strong and muscular.

"Alex, we'd like to take you to the hospital to get you checked out. Can we get you to go with us?" the officer asked.

"I'd rather not go."

"I can understand that, but we really need you to go with us. Just so we can get you checked out and make sure you are OK," one of the paramedics says in a voice that is smooth and calm.

"What if I don't want to go?"

"Well, we can make it so you do, but it would be much easier on everyone if you'd just agree to go to the hospital. Just so we can get you checked out."

Alex flashes one of his smiles that can melt your heart and says,

"OK, I'll go."

My chest feels as if it will burst, and my knees feel week as Alex climbs into the back of the ambulance on his own free will.

"Thank you," I whisper to Abba.

"Alex, Dad and I will be right there." The pleasantness in his voice returns, as he has one of the most normal conversations I have heard him have in days, with the EMT who is sitting beside him.

Quickly I text my sister to ask if she will come stay with Drew. He is still in an emotionally fragile state, and I do not feel safe leaving him alone.

After I have made arrangements, Jeff and I climb into our SUV and drive to the hospital. My prayer has changed. I am asking God to let the doctors see what they need to see from Alex. That Alex will not be able to pull himself together enough to fool them, as he has been able to do before. I send out a text to my prayer warriors and ask them to pray the same thing. As Jeff drives, I pray over and over and over, "Let them see what they need to see, Father. Let them see what they need to see. Let the see what they need to see. Let them see what they need to see."

Chapter Thirty-One

When we arrive at the hospital, Alex is in a bed in the hallway. Officer Vollmer and our friend Don are sitting beside him. Don's voice is calm and caring as he listens to Alex talk. Alex is pleasantly chatting away with these two men, the nurses, and anyone else who passes him. He is in full charm-them mode. He flashes a smile and his laughter floats around him like he is just sitting having a normal conversation on a normal day. I continue to pray, "Let them see what they need to see."

The hospital ER is overflowing with patients, all over the place waiting for an exam room. Alex is right beside the nurses' station, so they are frequently talking to him. I wonder how it is that he can be so seemingly normal in this moment when just an hour ago he was threatening to kill his brother and father. How is it that the evil which seems to lurk within him can be at bay at such an opportune moment?

"Father, let them see what they need to see."

Officer Vollmer stays for much longer than he is required. I mention to him several times how we appreciate his attention and help. He is quite humble and almost embarrassed that I have called attention to his kindness. He waits with us until, finally, several hours later, Alex is assigned to an exam room.

Almost as if someone has flipped a switch, Alex begins to not make as much sense. His speech becomes more agitated, his demeanor more panicked. It isn't as though all of the charm is gone, but the splattering of the psychosis is quickly filling the atmosphere. He is quickly assessed and then we wait, for hours we wait for someone from the psychiatric floor to do an assessment.

While we wait, Alex is becoming more agitated. He is doing push ups on the floor and the wall because he says it helps him to feel calm. He listens to the same song on his phone over and over and over. There are a few phone calls to Alex by people he has hung out with for the past few months. Names I don't even recognize; I flashback to a time when I knew the names of all of his friends and their parents. Those days are clearly gone.

The phone calls and subsequent conversations agitate Alex and increase his anxiety, which in turn increases the symptoms of psychosis. He becomes angry and raises his voice; he begins to beat the wall. The hospital staffer who has been assigned to watch Alex comes into his room to survey the situation. He tells Alex he must calm down. At this point, they tell him he can no longer have his cell phone, and he reacts much calmer than I anticipated, maybe because the food he has ordered from the hospital cafeteria arrives at about the same time, and he is quickly distracted. He is adamant about needing fish with lemon and black pepper. He tries to explain to me how the lemon and black pepper will help to remove the evil spirit that is within him. I try to listen and understand, but his speech is increasingly cryptic.

Shortly after this, someone comes in to discuss in further detail what is going on with Alex. As my son begins to speak, describing what is going on, I hit record on my cell phone and make a recording. I'm sure to hold the phone so it does not look like I'm recording him, but I feel this intense need to capture the utter confusion and chaos that is his speech.

What follows is a transcript of that recording. Some names have been changed.

His name is Father Dilly. I don't know, I don't know if he's Father Dilly. I just know that's the only thing to call him. I don't know what his last name is. He introduced himself and and basically that's all I remember yesterday. Not all, but the thing that's most prominent in my head with that exorcism, and the thing is…

"So how did you do the exorcism? I'm curious," the medical attendant asked.

He put on his purple priest whatever thing. He had holy water. He had his rosary. He had all the tools he needed. I was sitting down on just a couch; they didn't have me strapped down, so that's why I'm not sure if it was a real exorcism or not. I just know that the minute he said, let's open in a word of prayer, the first word he said my demons were right here. (Alex motions with clutched hands to his chest.)

And normally that would mean a blackout. I would start speaking in different, Latin, in dead languages I don't know how to speak, but I've spoken them. I've had friends say, friends that have sold their souls to the devil, say, "You just spoke in a language you should not have spoken." I looked at them and was like, "No, I just spoke in English." "No, you didn't."

The fear, the fear in their eyes. They don't get scared; they speak to Satan every day. Lucifer is manifest with them at all times. I feel Lucifer next to me when I'm next to these people. He was scared; he was very scared. I lost my train of thought where were we going?

"Exorcism," Jeff says.

Yah, yah, basically he he read a passage. When I talk to him I can get the passage if you're interested. I just know the minute it started happening I should have blacked out, but I didn't. I was totally aware, but I was paralyzed where I was, and I couldn't move. That's how I know this man knew what he was doing.

I don't really remember much of what he said because I was in so much pain. I want to say this prayer he was reading came straight out of the Bible. It was Old Testament. I know that because everything I saw in her was me completely being absolved of my sins, and God saying you are forgiven.

Once he started spraying holy water on me, I had my friend, who sold his soul to the devil, sitting next to me, right? He sprays this holy water, and it hits both of us. I don't move. My friend jumped about 10 feet in the air. I don't know if he left the room, but I think he couldn't. He was too interested in what was going on, but the holy water hit him, and I saw steam come off him as well. I know that as he did this, he's spraying holy water on me I'm like burning. I'm like seizing up. I should have been dead, and he finishes the prayer, and I just get this sigh of relief. Oh my God! I haven't been this mentally clear for three and a half years.

My friend committed suicide on November 14th, 2010, since then Rick Rex has been following me around. What I meant to tell you in the beginning, and I think I got sidetracked, maybe I was meaning to tell you guys this, (Alex looks at Jeff and me), but it is something she (he gestures towards the medical attendant) will want to hear too.

So, the first night he killed himself, I'm with my youth pastor Tom, and we're at church, and I'm with my friend Wayne, who's my blood brother by bonds not by blood. Him and I have had connections for years. A connection I can't spiritually talk to you about for his safety and my own. We both kind of look at each other while we're church, and we say where the f*** is Joe. He should be here right now, and it was at that exact moment he had died. I don't remember what time we thought that. I know that Tom and I were on our way home. He lives right next to me across the street a little bit. I know that we were on our way home by 8:30-9:00 because everybody was usually out of that church, whatever youth group, by that time.

So, we were on our way home on the road, but then we go down our road, Hilltop Road. I don't know if you're familiar with that, it's in Rochester, but we're going down, and I see an ambulance in our neighborhood. I've already had like hands around my heart, like something awful is about to happen, and once I saw that ambulance, my heart collapsed. I was like, oh, my God! It's Joe! Joe is in that ambulance.

When we get down the street, I see all the fire trucks, and and at first, I don't know what's going on. I'm like, oh, my God! My family is dead! Someone's dead! What's going on?! Now I know, no, I know; I don't know how I would have processed it, if I was in this state of mind. So we get there, (Alex's voice is breaking at this point, and he is holding back tears), and he parks out front, and he goes inside. He comes back out, and the look on his face, it's just like, you know. I, I couldn't know, but I was reading his thoughts back then, and I knew immediately.

I went home, and dad was the only one home. She was away (Alex motions towards me). Him and I have not had a good relationship for a long time, so I couldn't talk to him for a while. So I went down to my room, and I freaked out.

"You called me." I interject.

"Yah, so I'm in the first stage of grief, and I'm in denial. I get on the Internet, and I start seeing these posts. Rest in peace Joe Brady. RIP Joe Brady, blah, blah, blah.

The next day we go over there. This is where I have to stand up. (Alex stands up next to the hospital bed). I walk into the house, and I'll go into detail in a minute about the seances they used to do in this house, this was unbeknownst to me at the time, but I walk into this house, and immediately I'm hit with dark energy. There is an entire like hundreds of people in this house, anybody who is everybody, Rochester friends, kids, anybody. Everybody was in this house probably damn near two to three thousand people through it in a matter of a month span.

This first night, there were just a lot of people going in and out. When we walked in, it was basically an assembly line, and we assembly lined downstairs. You walk in this house, and there's a little bit of a hallway. You walk right to the parents' bedroom, and the washroom and out to the garage, or you go left to the stairs, where he hung himself.

I walk down the stairs. The minute my feet are in this house, I'm weak, and now I know what it is, but I'm weak and I'm walking. I take one step on the stairs, and I almost pass out, so I grabbed onto the railing and right then, like I know what it is. It was me feeling the energy, me figuring out, and me accepting that the Rick Rex demon needed somebody else to go into. It went into me. Thank God it was me and nobody else in that house. So I'm here, and I'm frozen on the wall and everybody thinks I'm just shaking because of the emotional everything.

What had happened to Joe was that approximately two months to just a month before he and a group of my riends had been playing songs backwards that shouldn't have been played backwards, Satanic rituals, seances in this house. Joe told my friend Alan, maybe a week, maybe month before he died, that he had seen Lucifer looking back at him in the mirror.

Depending on what demon this is, and I believe it is Rick Rex, if it's the demon I think it is. He has two horns coming out of his head. He's about 8ft. tall. He's big. He's scary. If you saw him and didn't know what you were looking at, you would think you were looking at Lucifer. My friend tells me this long after he's (Joe is) dead and he's emotional. This all just connected the last few days. This is how I got possessed the first time.

Anywhoo, so I'm in this house. I'm frozen, and I'm shaking, and I get thrown into Joe's body, you know when he died, and I'm cold as body. I'm on the very last step at the bottom, and the noose is around my neck. I feel the burning in the back of Joe's head that the demon was doing to him.

Here's the crazy thing. He didn't want to die. He wanted help, but he didn't know how to ask for help. He thought he had f***** up too bad. So I'm here in his body, the noose around his neck. The thing to keep in mind is Joe laid out every gun in his house. Every weapon was on his parents' bed. Anything he could have killed himself with. He was looking for options, He wanted to kill himself, but he didn't have the balls to do it. So, I'm in his body, the noose around my neck, and I feel the burning, and I feel Joe look up at where he had hung the noose.

The craziest thing was this banister wasn't strong enough. I mean this was a little boy, but but he was solid. He probably weighed about a hundred and fifty pounds, and in order to kill yourself right you're going to jump and snap your neck, so you don't feel the paint. Right. Right? (Alex looks at the medical attendant.)

"It depends on your choice," the attendant replies.

I meant it depends on your choice, absolutely. I'm in his body, noose around my neck burning, he looks up, he looks forward, and I feel the demon. Joe's right here, (Alex motions with his hands creating an imaginary person standing in front of him.) I'm the demon now, and I feel him go, (Alex raises his leg and kicks with all his might) kick him off. And when he gets kicked off, he's scratching the walls. The scratches are so deep and so painful for me to touch that night. He's scratching the walls, and he's trying to get back up, and the demon is just sitting there with nails dug into his shoulders, holding him, and choking him to death. Letting the noose do its job. And then it is gone, and I'm back to myself. And I walk downstairs, and you know I'm so emotionally wrecked and drained, I don't even know what I just saw.

I've never told anybody that except for you three in this room, and a few friends that I realized this with a few nights ago. This is what all is going on, and I mean all the dark energy is out of that house now. Now I know Joe's soul is okay. He didn't kill himself; he was executed by a demon. I believe that Joe, 'cause, I have a friend, I used to rap GD. If you know anything about gangs they're either Kalluminati or Illuminati . Illuminati worships the Devil. They pray to the devil; they do devilish things. Kalluminati is like GD; Gangster Disciples. They work for God, but they all do the same thing. It's just one more way to get spiritual warfare out there for people to catch; one more thing for us to kill each other over.

"Why don't you sit down buddy?" Jeff questions.
I can't. I can't.
"Aren't you tired?"
No, I can't.
"Okay. I just didn't know if you were getting tired."
No.
"Okay."

So, all this happens. All the dark energy is out of the house. I felt it. I don't know if they knew what happened, but they knew to get the house cleansed. I mean somebody, I don't remember who it is that's for Illuminati not Kalluminati; he came up to me and said, " We figured out what's wrong man."

I just got this Joe feeling, this Joe sense that I had, and I said, "No."

He said, "Yeah." Then told me.

And I was like, "No, you're…"

"Yeah, dude that was his demon."

And I was like, "Well that makes sense."

In Greenville, I don't know how many days or months it was before the first time I got admitted, and I had all this psychosis stuff.

Anywhoo, when that happened, unbeknownst to me, I came under another demonic possession. There was this girl who was my buddy's ex-girlfriend. She has, had, I have it now, a very, very powerful, very, very powerful sex demon. Either Incubus or succubus. I don't know. I've been told I have both. This was before this possession. My buddy Troy who trained me in the Arts, the dark arts that I'm aware of, that I learned when I was a Gangster Disciple running with them, he's with me. He came down to see me, and I basically said, "Bruh, you got to come see this b**** she is nuts. There's something spiritually wrong with her, and I want you to come tell me what the hell you think it is. I want to keep messing with it, but I can't. It's too powerful for me."

So, we get her; we're smoking weed in the graveyard, and I'm talking to her and come to find out this girl had been diagnosed with split personality disorder medically, but what it was was that she blacked out and a demon would be talking to her. Because in the car, we are smoking and everything's fine, and all of a sudden, he and I feel an energy shift. And her lights are on she is not home. Her voice changes, and she gets real sexual, very melodic, very satanic; the possession had taken control of her.

All this is going on, and she leans forward, and whispers in my ear. Now I know it's Latin, but at the time I didn't know it was Latin, but now I know it was Latin that sounded like English.

I feel tingling start at the tips of my toes. It was like dark energy coming up from my feet, and I feel like it got right below my heart. When this happened, immediately my friend grabs this girl's hand and takes it off, says something I don't remember, it was not of this language. She immediately snaps back and gets really hurt about what just happened.

She said, "Why did you do that? I was just trying to help him."

He snaps on her again, doesn't ever bring it up, and we go drop her off. And go talk about it.

He said, "Bro, she was downloading a demon into you."

I said, "What?"

He said, "That's exactly what was happening."

There's no way she got it, she got it into me, whether all the way or not, so to my knowledge, and I know this is a lot to take in, but to my knowledge, my purpose on this Earth is to collect demons that everybody has, so that I can communicate with people in ways that most people can't. I believe that the dark arts I have been trained in, I am allowed to use. It's Wicca Magic, which is very against the Christian religion and the Christian religion. But I believe because of my bloodline because of the things I have felt, the ways I have felt all this good stuff, I feel like I'm allowed to dabber in this, until I get to otherwise not to.

"Are you having any suicidal thoughts," the attendant questions.

No, ma'am. I've never been this not suicidal in my life.

"Any thoughts of hurting anybody?"

Yes and only because of this demonic s***, and now in this room? No, I never intentionally wanted to hurt anyone. I just told people, look at the bewitching hour you need to strap me down. I don't trust myself right now.

"Anyone in particular?"

That I've threatened?

"That you want to kill?" the attendant clarifies.

No, no. And that's the thing, I don't want to hurt anyone. I don't want to hurt anyone. I just want to help people.

"Did you make some threats to your parents?"

Absolutely. Lots of threats, I was angry. They stole a lot of drugs and money from me. I'm in trouble with a lot of people.

"Who stole drugs and money from you?"

Them (Alex gestures in Jeff's and my direction). They didn't steal it. It was their house. They had a right to take it. It's just now I'm in a shit lot of trouble with a lot of people.

"What kind of drugs other than marijuana?"

You guys found the fentanyl patch didn't you? (Alex asks Jeff and me.)

"Dad's the one that found the drugs," I answer.

Well maybe he didn't tell you about that. I don't know what all was in there. I just know that fentanyl patch. I had no idea what it was. Yeah, it was a fentanyl patch, the strongest opioid you can get to heroin addicts when they need painkillers.

"I destroyed all of it, okay," Jeff looks directly at the medical attendant.

"What else was in there?" She questions.

"Just drug paraphernalia."

"I mean there were no hard drugs?"

"Just marijuana, a fairly large amount of marijuana."

"I mean it kind of sounds like you guys are wanting him to be admitted. We don't have any beds here in Springfield, so what we'll do is try to find a bed for him outside the city not exactly sure where that will be," the attendant says apologetically.

Why are you admitting me without my permission?

"Well, you know it seems like things are a bit off..."

Absolutely, and I understand that, but I just really don't want to be admitted.

"...and sounds like you're not really able to control yourself when you're having these episodes of, and you just said you've had times where you've told people to strap you down because you didn't feel you could be trusted."

Can we talk on a one-on-one basis?

"Sure," the attendant says invitingly.

Ok, everything I told is of the last few days, and the minute that priest blessed me and got me under control, I've been mentally clear. I've been revoking my own demons. I need no one's help revoking my own demons. Now the only help I need is from a priest to trained me how to when I get a demon out of someone, I don't know what to do with it, so I throw it away, but I don't know how to bind it. And in order to perform the the exorcism, you have to bind the spirit to something or it will come back. So I want to hurt no one. I will hurt no one. Ask them (Alex motions to Jeff and me), they heard the conversation I had with my buddy. I'm going to his house, so that he can make sure I hurt no one. This is my friend who is trained in the dark arts. He can control my demons just as well as I can control my demons.

"You see the thing is I don't know that much about the dark arts," the attendant admits.

I'm aware of that and this is hard to believe. I just can't get admitted.

"My thing is I have to make sure that you're safe and your family is safe."

Yes, ma'am. I understand that, but I cannot be admitted tonight.

"And that's where we're at."

So how do I convince you that I can't be admitted tonight?

"Pardon me?" She says.

How do I convince you that I can't be admitted tonight?

"I don't think you can," she gently replies.

How are you going to admit me without my permission, when I'm 18 years old? This is against the law.

"You're 18 years old, but you can be admitted as an involuntary patient, if you're not agreeable to it..."

For how long?

"...if we feel you are a danger to yourself or others." (Alex is becoming visibly upset.)

"Just let it, just let it," Jeff says to Alex quietly,

I'll let it when it's cooler, I'm trying to figure out.

"We need to see if it works. We have gotta try something. We gotta try something different, dude, and see if it works," Jeff pleads with Alex.

"Buddy," I begin.

No, no, there is no buddy, you pissed me off again. 'Cause now I'm getting admitted for goddamn nothing.

I quickly stop recording because Alex is getting angrier with each breath, and I don't want him to know I've been recording.

Even though Jeff and I breathe a small sigh of relief knowing the hospital will admit Alex, it isn't something that either of us ever wanted. The realization of what is happening mixed with complete exhaustion hits us. I step out of the room and quickly walk to the nearest restroom. The tears are coming faster and faster, and as I close the door, I can barely see the lock on the door.

Chapter Thirty-Two

A couple more hours pass and finally a doctor from the psychiatric floor comes to examine Alex. This doctor says that Alex will definitely be admitted and that the nurses are calling to find a bed for him. The doctor has no comforting words to give us in reference to how long it will take to find an available bed. It is approaching 1 a.m. The wait is excruciating. It is mixed with more terrifying talk from Alex mixed with anger and agitation.

"I think we need to go home and try to get some rest. Alex is safe here. There is nothing we can do to speed things up by waiting here," Jeff says gently.

My heart sinks. How can I leave my baby in this desperate time of need? A panic begins to wrap around my throat, and my heart begins to beat fast and heavy in my chest. My mind is racing to think, but my brain isn't working well. Exhaustion is engulfing me, and I don't have the energy to even argue with Jeff. The nurse assures me she will call if anything changes or when a bed is found for Alex, so I agree to leave.

At almost 3 a.m., we fall into bed. Three and a half short hours later, I am jolted from my sleep by my alarm. Because I am a public speaking teacher and my students are scheduled to give major speeches today, I do not allow myself to call a substitute teacher. It wouldn't be fair to the kids. Pushing back their speeches to another day, could compromise their readiness.

I stumble out of bed and check my phone for messages, nothing. I step into the shower, and the water wakes me up, but my heart still feels so heavy. My lungs aren't working very well. Tears are streaming down my face as I realize that the prayer I had been praying 12 hours ago was answered. The doctors did see what they needed to see. It was obvious that Alex needed serious help. There was no question about admitting him.

"Thank you, God! Thank you for being here with us in the midst of this very, very dark place. You are moving! I see you moving! Bring healing, Father! Healing to my Alex! Father, we need a bed for Alex. We need a place for him to be admitted. God, I am asking you to create a place for him right here in Springfield. A bed right here in Springfield, God. That is what I am asking for right now. Father, if that is not in your will, please create a space for him where you know he will get the help he needs with the doctors you already know are the best doctors for correctly treating him. I trust you Lord. I trust you."

Chapter Thirty-Three

I call the hospital as I am driving to work. No bed has been found, but the nurses are waiting on a call from a facility in Peoria, and they are hopeful.

"Father, your will be done."

After finishing my first two morning classes, I leave the building immediately. Knowing if I hurry, I can run to the hospital and check in on Alex before heading to my next school and class of students.

When I get to the hospital, Alex has been moved to a room at the back of the ER, a room with fewer distractions from the normal hustle and bustle. He is under 24- hour observation. I recognize his voice before I see him. He is really angry.

"I want you to contact our lawyer and sue this hospital. They just gave me drugs when I refused them. They held me down and shot me with some sort of poison," he is sobbing now. "That f****** nurse told them to do it. Call our lawyer. Will you call him now?! I want to talk to him NOW!"

"Alex, honey, I'm sure they need you to calm down. You cannot be yelling," I try to soothe. "I'll make some notes, so I remember what to tell the lawyer," I stall.

"I wouldn't be yelling if they hadn't just given me God knows what. All I was doing was pushups on the wall trying to calm myself, so maybe I could sleep, and that b**** came in here and told them to hold me down and drug me." He escalates quickly. He punches walls, kicks over a tray and sobs.

"Why do I want to kill myself? What's wrong with me?"

I pray over him and he becomes calmer for a few moments, but the agitations returns. He begins to writhe in pain, and as he is flopping his body back and forth he beings to hyperventilate.

A nurse walks in and, judging from her demeanor, it is the nurse to whom Alex is referring.

"Mr. Davis, if you do not stop becoming violent and disruptive, I am going to have the attendant hold you down and administer something else. You need to stop yelling."

"He is really sick and confused right now. I'll help him calm down," I say as emphatically as

I can. I look in her eyes and wonder if she is a mother too, hoping for just a moment she could see past the anger and confusion and witness the sweet boy who is trapped behind it all, and the momma whose heart is fighting to help him break free.

I am able to talk Alex into lying down, and I can tell whatever they have given him is starting to calm him. His breathing is slowing; his tension seems to be lessening. It has been over two weeks since he has slept. The psychotic episode is doing its thing. He desperately needs sleep, but the longer he goes without sleep, the more difficult it becomes for him to sleep, a terrifyingly familiar cycle. I want to wrap him up in my arms and rock him, as I did so many times when he was a baby, but healing this sickness will take more than what I can offer.

The clock is ticking, and I have to head to my next school to teach. Before I go, I speak to the nurse, trying to replace the hostility she was showing with some tenderness. I tell her how long we have been fighting this battle, how it has stolen my baby, and I see her face soften. I apologize for Alex's behavior and assure her that if she met him when he was well, she would love him. Just before I go, a phone call comes in. A bed has been found for Alex at the very hospital he is currently in. This is just another one of those moments when God makes sure that I know He is in control.

When I get back to the hospital, it is about 3:30. Alex has been in the ER for 21 hours. He tells me they are about to move him to his room, but I sit and wait with him for over two hours before someone actually comes.

By the time we are moving to the Psychiatric Ward, Alex's speech has become slurred. He is slumped in the wheelchair. Whatever medicine they have given him is taking its toll. As we enter through one locked hallway after another, my panic is increasing. What have I done? They are locking my baby away in this horrible place. The scene looked just like what I've seen in movies, people shuffling around and talking to themselves. Someone is softly banging his head on the wall, someone else yells as we walk by; a group of people is sitting at tables coloring with crayons. I am so thankful that Alex is out of it; this would surely increase his agitation.

Alex's sleepiness doesn't last long, and he starts to become agitated again. He makes it clear to the medical staff that he will NOT take any medication they want to give him. As he takes a much-needed shower, I wait in the hallway pacing back and forth. I send a text out to update my prayer warriors, asking for prayer that Alex be willing to take whatever medication the hospital wants to give him. When he comes out of the shower, for just a moment I see the smile that makes my heart want to explode with happiness, but it is just a flash and is quickly replaced with more delusion.

May 30, 2014, 6:51 a.m.—text to prayer warriors

Today I ask that you pray that Alex will take his Antipsychotic medicine whatever that may be. That God will remove his aversion to taking these medications. That he will hear LOUDLY AND CLEARLY that it is Satan that wants to keep him sick and have him not take the medicine. God wants him well!! And to be well he MUST take these medicines and he MUST continue to take them.

10:59 a.m.—text to prayer warriors

He took the meds!!!!!!!!! And he says he will continue!!!! Thank you, Jesus.

June 1, 2014, 1:12 pm—text to prayer warriors

Alex is doing better, but he has a long road to be who he is supposed to be. Please pray that he will hear God's voice and be obedient. That he will be drawn to people who are filled with light and stay AWAY from the darkness.

June 2, 2014, 8:06 p.m.—text to prayer warriors

Saw Alex today. He is talking in all directions wanting to do the right thing one minute but talking about doing the wrong things the next minute. He has a lot of confusion and is still tormented by many things. He needs clarity in thought and clear direction. He needs to hear the voice of God reminding him God wants him well. He needs peace to sleep. He needs to feel protected by warrior angels. He needs resolve to stop doing the things that aren't holy and good. Please keep praying. He is still taking the meds, which is a praise. He seemed so confused and scattered today.

He calls me at all hours, even when I am at school and supposed to be teaching. I always answer. One day he called as I walked from the library to my classroom.

"Hi, Momma. How are you today?"

"I'm OK. How are you?"

"When are you getting me out of here? I need to get out. Will you talk to the doctors and tell them to let me leave? It is horrible in here. People are screaming and yelling at things that aren't there. The person next to me is ranting about a spirit being in her room, and she does this all hours of the night. I cannot sleep. I cannot think."

"Alex, you have to do what the doctors say. You have to take the medicine."

"If you don't get me out of here, I'm going to kill myself. And it will be all your fault."

I am huddled in a corner in the hallway. As I cup my hand around the phone, in an attempt to amplify Alex's voice, I can feel my chest tighten and my heart speed up. Students are busily talking and passing me by, unaware of the weight of the moment I am experiencing. I tell my brain to tell my lungs to breathe in and out, but there is a miscommunication as my lungs don't respond.

Zzzzzzz- the sound of the tardy bell blasts through the hallways

"Alex, honey. Please don't say that. I love you. I'm so sorry, but I have to go. I love you."

"You don't love me! If you loved me, you'd TAKE ME OUT OF HERE!! You'd tell the doctors I'm NOT SICK!!! When something happens to me, remember, it is YOUR F***** FAULT!!"

"I love you," I whisper and disconnect the call. It is a good thing I am so close to a wall, because it is what holds me up, as I take a deep breath, wipe my tear-drenched face, and tell myself to pull it together. I have a classroom of students waiting for me.

As I walk into the room, the students are none the wiser. I'm getting pretty good at pretending to be OK.

Chapter Thirty-Four

More time passes, and Alex continues to go up and down. Visiting him is difficult because he becomes angry and agitated. He talks in every direction about everything and nothing at the same time. It is exhausting to visit him, but we keep going. The doctors want to have a family session to discuss Alex going into rehab, but Alex doesn't seem too interested in this.

Alex has been in the hospital for 11 days. He seems slightly better, but there is no denying evil is present. It seems that the stress of the hospital unit and the evil that I know is there is really not helpful for Alex's healing. It is as if he is being constantly attacked. He does well when he has people there with him praying protection over him, but when we leave, or whoever has been with him leaves, he is swarmed by the attacker again. I am nervous about what will happen. Will he continue taking the meds? Will he go right back to where he was before? I don't have answers, but I'm wondering if his staying in the hospital any longer is going to help much more. He needs therapy, to be away from the other patients and hopefully to get back to church.

We are scheduled to meet with the doctors from the hospital. The day before, I ask our prayer warriors to join us at our house to pray with us. About 10 of our friends and family join us, and, again, we gather around our 100-year-old dining room table. We ask for direction, for wisdom, for Alex to be willing to take the antipsychotic medication, for God to intervene and make Alex well.

June 9, 2014, 11:42 a.m.-text to prayer warriors

Our God is an AWESOME GOD!!!!! After a HORRIBLE beginning to our last meeting (lasted 2hrs), which included Alex ranting most of the time, the conversation turned. Alex broke down, Jeff broke down, and then Alex became more rational and was able to talk AND listen. And he AGREED to take the antipsychotic medication!!!! Ask and you will receive! Thank you, Lord Jesus!!!!!

Two days after Alex agrees to take the antipsychotic medication, his doctor says he is doing much better. The staff is reporting that he is more appropriately involved in conversations and activities. The doctor is hoping Alex will be discharged by the end of the week. But we all know the hard work will begin once he leaves the hospital. It is key that he gets connected with the right professionals, adults, and peers, stays away from street drugs, and continues to take the medication. Many prayers are still needed, but things are definitely improving.

June 12, 2014, 2:19 p.m.-text to prayer warriors

Alex will be discharged tomorrow morning. We are thankful, nervous, and hopeful. He will have a long road of recovery ahead of him, if he chooses to take it. We pray he does. We pray he gets connected with the right people both professionally and socially. We pray he stays on his medicine and stays away from street drugs. And Jeff and I pray for wisdom to know and strength to do whatever it is God wants us to do to help Alex in this journey. We will continue to need prayers on a daily basis. Thank you all for all you have done on our behalf already. We are strengthened by it.

After Alex is released from the hospital, things are calm. He sees his psychiatrist just a few hours after leaving the hospital and says he will continue to take the meds because he knows he needs them. I am hesitantly hopeful. The sweetness that is Alex peeks through more and more with each passing day. He asks Jeff and me to go with him to both Rochester Christian Church and Calvary Church on Sunday morning. This is a miracle!

Chapter Thirty-Five

June 15, 2014 4:45pm—text to prayer warriors

Just to share some YEAH GOD moments. We went as a family to Rochester Christian this morning, and then Jeff, Alex, and I went to Calvary's young adult service. The sermon was Spirit inspired. The speaker said he had preached at the previous two services but was being told by the Holy Spirit to give his testimony because God was telling him that someone who was present needed to hear it. WOW! God knew Alex was coming to that service. It was one of those times when the power, plan, wisdom, and love of God were nothing less than overwhelming. Alex went forward for prayer, and it was POWERFUL!! He ended up meeting some of the young adult leaders, and they shared phone numbers and invited him to all kinds of activities. It was overwhelmingly GOD!!

June 23, 2:41pm—text to prayer warriors

Just an update on our lives, Alex is getting better each day-slowly. He is still taking his meds and going to regular check-ups with his psychiatrist. He starts seeing a therapist this week. He also started working out this week and will begin seeing a physical therapist for his back (another reason he was self-medicating before) in hopes of getting the pain in check. We still need prayer specifically for the following things: Alex is having an extremely hard time getting into a regular sleep schedule; he wakes up VERY irritable and angry, and he is trying to get a job; he is trying to get physically fit, and he is trying to stop smoking (has replaced with chew…ugh!). He continues to say he has not used any street drugs since he got out of the hospital. I can only pray that is true, and he continues to desire to do so. He needs to have the motivation to surround himself with good things and people, needs to be willing to make the effort to do what he knows he should be doing. And for both boys, please pray that God will give them discernment to know what they are to do as they venture into adulthood. Our home becomes more peaceful each day. We are thankful for your continued prayer and support as we ask for this to continue.

Things continue to move forward in a positive direction. Drew is able to get caught up with the schoolwork he missed and is enjoying the summer before his senior year of high school. We were starting to feel as though we could breathe and actually have some moments of fun.

On July 4, 2014, we celebrated the holiday like many: pool party, food, and friends. In the midst of the party, Alex asked if he could talk to

234

me. Something in his demeanor told me this was something I wasn't going to like.

"I am going to stop taking my medicine," he said. "I feel that I need to give God a chance to heal me."

"What? Stop taking your medicine? Alex, you are just starting to get really balanced," I say, a panic mixed with pride swirling inside my chest.

"Mom, if I don't stop taking the medicine, how can God heal me? I feel like I have to trust Him and give Him a chance to do so."

"There is nothing our God cannot do! But the medicine is one thing God is using to help you get well, Alex. I really admire your desire to trust Him, but I just don't know if the timing is right," I say as I begin to pray in my mind for wisdom and the correct words as I speak to Alex. There is NO DOUBT in my mind that God can heal Alex, so my guilt at questioning Alex's desire to step out is matched only by my panic. It hasn't been long since he has been able to hold a sane conversation while on medication this time. We have been here before; flashes of last year flicker through my memory. The emotional wounds of the on again off again battle that was fought with Alex over medication just a year ago

235

are still so fresh. I realize that whether he takes the medication or not is yet another thing I do not control. As my guests splash and laugh and celebrate, I pray, and I sing, and I pray.

A few weeks later, Alex and I are heading to a Christian concert at Six Flags in St. Louis, Missouri. As we drive, we listen to one of my favorite stations, 99.1 Joy FM. Alex and I sing as we drive. My heart is overflowing with gratitude. It has been four weeks since he decided to stop taking the medicine, and things are still moving slowly forward.

It is a HOT day in St. Louis, and the concert is held outdoors, but that does not stop us from celebrating as we praise our God. Alex stood with hands raised, eyes closed, and sang and praised. So many times, I was brought to tears as flashes of what we had been through, so much fear, so much sadness, so much hoping for a better tomorrow, passed through my mind. Here I was standing with my prodigal son at a Christian concert worshiping God; my thankfulness was immeasurable.

It was so incredibly hot that night, and as Alex went to fetch drinks for us, the woman who sat beside me at the concert leaned over to speak to me.

"I've been watching your son, watching him sing and praise God. If every teen was like him, there would be no problems in the world," she said with a sadness in her eyes.

"Thank you," I said, stunned that she had noticed. "If I told you his story, you wouldn't even believe it. Keep praying for your own teens. There is so much power in prayer," I assured her.

Alex returned with the drinks, and she leaned over to speak to him.

"I'm really impressed by how you are not embarrassed to raise your hands and sing and praise God. There aren't a lot of teens who would do that in public."

Alex said something to her; I couldn't hear what he said, but the next thing I knew they were hugging each other. Is our God great or what? It is another reminder that he is working everything out for His good.

In the fall, we attend another concert. This one was Big Daddy Weave. It is, again, an amazing experience with my Alex. We sing and we praise and have an awesome time together. One of the things Mike Weaver is passionate about is supporting children through monthly financial support and prayer in foreign countries. It is at this concert that I watch my 17-year-old son "adopt" his first child.

When the concert was over, Mike Weaver was standing greeting people. Alex and I stood in line with everyone else, watching as they took selfies with the singer. When it was our turn, I watched Alex and Mike talk. Mike couldn't stop looking into Alex's eyes. He seemed overwhelmed by what God was revealing to him about Alex.

"Man, there is something in your eyes, something really special. I'm not sure what it is, but God is going to do something really amazing with you!" Mike said as he smiled.

"I've had a pretty rough road lately," Alex replied.

Mike shook his head, "There is something about you."

"Can I take your picture?" I asked Mike as he stood with Alex.

They stood close together and Mike put his arm around Alex, and when the photo was over he took Alex's phone out of Alex's hand and texted himself.

"I want to keep updated on you," Mike said as he continued to look into Alex's eyes and smile.

I was witnessing something God was doing. I wasn't sure what, but I knew in that moment that God was giving me a glimpse of what was to come. I felt so sure that everything was going to be OK. There was a peace deep in the fibers of my soul that reminded me that God could be trusted even when nothing made sense. This was just one of the MANY times God gave me tangible evidence, so I could keep moving forward when it got bad again.

Chapter Thirty-Six

May 26, 2015 4:42 pm—text to prayer warriors

I am once again asking for prayer for my Alex. I started noticing symptoms of mania a few weeks ago, and they are getting worse. I have spoken to him about going to see his psychiatrist and get back on meds just to get himself balanced again. He listened and agreed that he didn't want to end up where he was last year, but so far he doesn't want to go see his doctor. Please join me in praying that God will convince Alex to get help before this gets any worse. I'm sure you can understand my panic is just under the surface. I KNOW Alex has been healed of so much; the fact that he has been off meds since last July 4 is a miracle in and of itself. He told me he feels like he is being unfaithful if he thinks about not being healed completely. I tried to assure him God doesn't look at it this way. Satan is crafty and will use anything to bring us down. But our God is mighty!!

"In this you greatly rejoice, though now for a little while you may have had to suffer grief in all kinds of trials. These have come so that your faith-may be proved genuine and may result in praise, glory, and honor when Jesus Christ is revealed."   --1 Peter 1:6-7

Alex begins to go back to many of his old patterns. He doesn't come home every night anymore, nor is he spending time with his Christian friends. Names of people from his past pop up in conversation, and all I can do is pray. I suspect that he may be using drugs again; however, I'm not sure if it is that or the fact that he isn't on medication.

"Father, give me wisdom."

One night I am driving back from a trip to see family in Southern Illinois, and I receive a phone call from Alex.

"Hi, Momma. How was your day?"

"Nice. I'm driving back from Murphysboro right now. Aunt Gabbi is in the car with me. How was your day?"

"Well, ummm, I wrecked my bike today," he says laughing.

"You wrecked your bike?!"

"Yep," he says with more laughter.

"Oh, my God, are you OK?"

"Yah, I'm fine. My bike isn't though," more laughter.

"Were you wearing your helmet?"

"Nope."

"What happened?"

"I was following a friend, and she turned left at an intersection, and I saw the light turning yellow, so I gunned it. I knew I was going down before it happened. I was trying to figure out how to fall and not get hurt. I knew my head was going to hit the pavement, but just as it should have hit the pavement, I felt a hand cup the back of my head. There were two off duty EMTs and one nurse at the intersection. They all jumped out of their vehicles and came to me. They were telling me not to move, and I put my hand at the back of my head thinking there should be blood all over the place, but there was nothing, so I stood up. I have some scrapes on my arm and leg but nothing else. One of the people at the intersection convinced me to go to the ER just to be sure everything was OK," he laughs again.

Tears are falling so fast, I can almost not see to drive. This could have been a very different phone call and the reality of this shakes me to the core.

"I'm so thankful you are OK," I am barely able to choke out the words.

Alex's mania is getting worse, but I still know God has a big plan for him. My prayer warriors continue to pray and some reach out to talk to him or meet with him. The Sunday following his accident, he attends two church services at Calvary Church. Even as his mind becomes more and more confused with the mania, he is a very thankful boy.

Chapter Thirty-Seven

June 30, 2015 1:16pm—text to prayer warriors

A prayer request: We are at the point where Alex needs to be on medication again. His mania is increasing in severity with his words, and some actions, becoming more and more outrageous. He is once again adamant that he does not want to take the medication. Please be praying specifically that he will feel the Holy Spirit prompting him to take the medicine as a way to get healthy. Those of you who have been praying for my Alex know we have witnessed several miracles over the last few years. We have witnessed the power of our almighty God. Please join with me in asking for HIS power to be shown again and all glory to go to HIM!!

July 3, 2015 1:06pm—text to prayer warriors

Alex asked me last night to contact his psychiatrist. He said he needs to be on the medicine. He will start taking the meds tonight. It will take some time for them to get into his system and for the medicine to start working. Of course the praise is that the Holy Spirit did speak loudly to Alex, and he chose to obey! GOD IS SO SO GOOD!! Thank you for the prayers you lifted on our behalf. Keep them coming! We had a really good talk two nights ago, and he said that he would at least be willing to consider the medicine. I told him he does not get to choose how God makes him or what God uses to make him well. He finally agreed I was right.

July 29, 2015 11:44 am—text to prayer warriors

An update on my family: Alex is more stable each day and continues to take his meds. PRAISE GOD!!! He is still talking about applying to that ministry training school in California and going in the fall; although he now says he thinks maybe God wants him to wait to go, but he thinks he still needs to apply. I am praying hard that God will truly be in that and put up a mountain to stop Alex if he is not to go. He is till working very part time as a host at Engrained Brewery, and he is very involved with Calvary Church. He is looking for another part time job, but he is either home, at work, or at church; all good signs. Drew is doing well.

Aug. 2, 2015, 6:02pm—text to prayer warriors

Update on Drew. We saw the new adult psychiatrist on Friday. The decision was made to attempt to take Drew off the Abilify again. (This was the medicine that the doctor took him off, and it caused the psychotic episode that landed him in the hospital last year.) This time they are starting Drew on a new medicine as they are taking him off the Abilify.

I must admit we are apprehensive about this because twice he has tried to get off this medicine and twice we have had very negative effects; however, it is truly in Drew's best interest to be off this medicine if at all possible. (It has caused major weight gain, high cholesterol, and he is now pre-diabetic). Plus, Drew is starting classes at LLCC in August, so he needs to be emotionally stable to do so. We feel that God led us to this doctor, and we know HE IS IN CONTROL. Please pray with us about this. We pray for a seamless transition off the Abilify and onto the new medication, and for Drew to not experience what he did before. Thank you again for continued support of prayer.

By the end of August, decided, at least for now, that he was not supposed to go to Bethel (the school in California). As he tried multiple times to electronically submit his application, it wouldn't go through. On his final attempt, he prayed that if God wanted him to go, the application would go through. It did not.

The next day, Alex and I talk for a long time about how he wants to get stronger in his faith and learn more about God and get into The Word. We talk a lot about how far he has come and what we have been through over the last five years.

Alex has been clean (again) for about three months and is fervently seeking God. He says this time it is very different.

It is in this conversation that he also tells me that he has stopped his medication again. I leave this, too, in the mighty hands of God.

Drew also continues to improve. He has recently been switched to a new medication, but we have seen ABSOLUTELY no change in his mood. This is a fantastic thing, and we are so thankful to God!

The doctor continues to take Drew off one medicine and increase the other. This process will take months. We continue to pray about this, asking God to keep Drew mentally and emotionally stable through this process.

Life is peaceful. Alex is immersing himself in everything positive. He hangs with his church friends most of the time. He is also helping with the youth group at Calvary Church, and is involved in a Bible study. The people in the Bible study have scooped Alex up and are spending a lot of time mentoring him. Alex is beginning to have some pretty amazing experiences with God as he trusts more and more.

"Because we know that this extraordinary day is just ahead, we pray for you all the time- pray that our God will make you fit for what he's called you to be, pray that he'll fill your good ideas and acts of faith with his own energy so that it all amounts to something. If your life honors the name of Jesus, He will honor you. God is behind and through all of this, our God giving himself freely, the master, Jesus Christ, giving himself freely." -- 2 Thessalonians 1; 11-2

Chapter Thirty-Eight

One night at youth group, Alex was standing back watching students go forward asking for prayer. When one student came up to Alex and asked him to pray for him, he did. Words that were divinely sent came from his mouth as he prayed about things this student was doing, things that didn't please God. As Alex continued to pray, he himself wasn't even sure what it all meant, but he prayed and continued to let the Holy Spirit work through him.

When the prayer was over, the student stepped away, and Alex stepped back to watch the other students being prayed over. The evening was over and the students were dismissed, but the student with whom Alex had prayed was waiting at the back of the church for him.

"How did you know to pray about that stuff?" the student questioned.

"I'm not really sure. I just started praying, and it all just came to me," Alex said smiling in disbelief, but recognizing the prayer had hit a cord.

"Were you watching me at the fair last year?"

"No," Alex laughed. "God told me what to pray."

About a week or so later, Alex received a phone call from this student's parents. Their son had told them about Alex, and they wanted to meet with him. Alex agreed to meet with them for lunch. During this meeting, the parents questioned Alex about the prayer. They wanted to know how Alex knew to pray about such things, the very things with which they were watching their son struggle?

Alex explained that he really doesn't know their son very well, but the prayer was a God moment. He then learned that the student's dad was a former detective and was quite suspicious of Alex, but they were seriously concerned about their son and the direction he was going. After talking to Alex and learning about his story, the parents asked him if he would be willing to spend time, to mentor their son. Alex agreed.

'For I know the plans I have for you, declares the Lord, plans to prosper you and not to harm you, plans to give you hope and a future. Then you will call upon me and come and pray to me, and I will listen to you. You will seek me and find me when you seek me with all your heart."

--Jeremiah 29:22.

A few weeks later, as Alex walked into the gym, God told him to go pray with this lady. She is a total stranger, and Alex shakes the thought off and goes to work out himself, but he cannot escape it.

"Go pray with her," he keeps hearing across the ticker of his mind.

He takes a deep breath, steps off his machine, and walks over to this lady.

"Hi. Umm I know this is weird, but can I pray with you?'

"Umm, OK," she replied with a look of confusion and surprise across her face.
Alex took a deep breath and put his hand on her shoulder, and as he began to pray, God revealed things about this woman and had Alex speak about things of which he couldn't possibly have knowledge. By the time he was done praying, the woman was crying.

"How did you know that about me? How did you know I needed someone to pray about that?" she asked with tears running down her face.

"God, He told me to pray with you, so I did."

"Wow," was her only reply.

253

Another time, Alex had a dentist appointment, and he felt God telling him to pray with the hygienist. The usual hygienist was out sick, so this lady is a sub for the day. As she is cleaning Alex's teeth, he can again hear God saying, "Pray with her."

"Would you be willing to let me pray with you?" Alex asked her.

She drew back from him, looked him in the eyes, and immediately tears began to form in her eyes. Then she shook her head yes. As Alex prayed, again God revealed to him challenges she was going through, things heavy on her heart, places where she needed to hear God's voice.

"How amazing that God knew you'd be my patient today! How did you know to pray for those things?"

"I don't really know what else to say, except God told me to pray with you, and then told me what to pray about," Alex answered with a smile.

Chapter Thirty-Nine

Jan. 10, 2016, 9:36 pm-a text to prayer warriors

I found out two days ago that Alex is
hanging out with one of his old friends.
I have voiced my concern and reminded him
that Satan isn't finished with him yet.
He knows Alex's weakness is his friends.
Please pray that Alex will be protected
from attacks from Satan, that Alex will
be strong against temptation, and that he
will immerse himself in prayer and
continue to seek the Holy Spirit's
presence. And I ask for peace for Jeff
and me…it's been a long, scary road, and
we don't want to go down it again.

January 29, 2016

We are heading in a terrifyingly familiar
direction, yet again. Little hints that Alex isn't
moving in the same direction as before. He is
hanging out once again with friends from his past.
Alex is distancing himself from church friends,
church activities, even family somewhat. He is
not coming home until late, and Jeff and I are
both in bed, so we never see him. I hear a train
whistle in the background outside as I write this.
It is like a warning to move. Why, Alex, are you
doing this again? Why can you not see this

pattern? It is a slow fade from where you are to where you do not want to be.

One day I finally do catch up with Alex and these words flow out.

"Here's what I know. The enemy will take any opportunity to sneak his way into our lives. He doesn't actually need an invitation to do so. All we have to do is open the door by the actions we choose or don't choose or the company we keep or don't keep. Satan wants to make your purpose on this Earth ineffective, Alex. He knows he cannot destroy you; you have already been won by Jesus, but Satan will work very hard to distract you from what your God-given purpose is. And after he has lured you away, he wants to suffocate you with guilt, insecurity, and fear. Satan is sneaky. He can drag you away before you even know it," I say.

He listens, and tells me I have nothing to worry about.

"I hope so," I whisper, more to myself than to him.

"Blessed is the man who perseveres under trial, because when he has stood the test, he will receive the crown of life that God has promised to those who love Him." ---James 1:12

Chapter Forty

The rest of 2016 was a lot of back and forth. It was obvious that Alex was making a concerted effort to stay away from his old habits, but he had a hard time staying away from his old friends. I could see him trying to make different choices, and I prayed that this time it was for real.

In November 2016, Alex attended the *Awake To Destiny Conference* in Champaign, Illinois and felt God telling him to apply to Bethel, the school in California, again. When Alex tells me this, I'd be lying if I said I wasn't nervous about this possibility. Again, I reminded myself that God knew what he was doing, and if he wanted or didn't want Alex at Bethel, He would make it so. Unlike the application that Alex tried to submit in 2015, this time he completed the questions and the application process with ease and submitted his application without any complications.

After a few weeks, Alex received an email confirmation that he was indeed accepted into Bethel School of Supernatural Ministry (BSSM) in Redding, California. Shortly after this, he received a phone call from Willy Bowles, founder and leader at the school. He explained to Alex that the staff had been praying about the incoming first year students, and God highlighted his name to them. Willy told Alex that they wanted to offer him the option of coming to the BSSD campus (Bethel School of Supernatural Discipleship) in Eureka, CA. instead because God had made it clear to them that he was to come to this campus and complete the program there.

After the shock of his plans being changed settled a bit, Alex and I began to pray. We prayed for direction. We prayed for the faith to jump where God was saying to jump. We prayed for peace to guide the decision that Alex would make. Shortly after this time, Alex made the commitment to attend BSSD in the fall of 2017 as a first-year student.

The summer was spent planning and purchasing the things Alex would need to move to California, live in an apartment, and attend BSSD. My heart was a mixture of joy and grief. I was overwhelmed with the thoughts of Alex beginning this part of his journey with God, and I was working hard not to focus on the coming absence of his physical presence in my daily life.

"Young men, in the same way be submissive to those who are older. All of you, clothe yourselves with humility toward one another, because 'God opposes the proud but give grace to the humble.' Humble yourselves, therefore, under God's mighty hand, that he may lift you up in due time. Cast all your anxiety on him because he cares for you. Be self-controlled and alert. Your enemy the devil prowls around like a roaring lion looking for someone to devour. Resist in Him, stand firm in the faith, because you know that your brothers throughout the world are undergoing the same kind of sufferings. And the God of all grace, who called you to his eternal glory in Christ, after you have suffered a little while, will himself restore you and make you strong, firm and steadfast."

--1 Peter 5:5-10

August 17, 2017

I am encompassed by overwhelming gratitude for what He has done, for where we are, for where God has taken us, where He has taken Alex. So often I find myself crying with thankfulness; how frightening this journey has been, but God's presence has been so close. Alex leaves for Bethel School of Discipleship in Eureka, CA. on August 30. We plan to drive together to Eureka. I'm so looking forward to this time together, just my boy and I.

I find myself fighting a sadness at one level; he will be so far away from home, and I will miss him so, and an overwhelming joy on another level when I think of where we have been and where we are now. How can I not fall at the feet of Jesus in gratitude for His grace, His mercy? I still don't know where God is taking Alex, but I know HE is in control.

Alex is wholly open to God's will for his life now. People have asked me if I am anxious for Alex to be so far. My thoughts go here. If God protected Alex in those DARK DAYS, He will continue to protect Alex. The only reason Alex is alive today is because of the hand of God.

"God, please know my heart. My tears are of a mother's heart in knowing my son will be so far away from me. Please don't mistake my tears for lack of gratitude for the miracles I have witnessed. You are a good God. Through it all, you have been so good."

Chapter Forty-One

August 30, 2017

Before the birds begin to sing, it is time for me to get up. I had not slept much but instead prayed my night away. My prayers last night were different than the countless prayers I had offered up over the last seven years. Last night, they were prayers of all-encompassing gratitude and praise. I didn't pray that God would tell me how to save my baby or to show me where he was because I didn't have to. I knew that God had brought us through searing pain and crippling fear to a place where the good stuff was going to really begin.

I had known all along that God would bring Alex through this, and it was at this moment that I could stand on the mountain and look back at the destruction of the valley through which we had passed. Passed. We had passed through the darkest valley. We had battled demons. We had battled addiction. We had battled depression, mental illness, suicide, and family strongholds. We had fought with principalities not of this world, and God had protected us at every single turn. He had indeed delivered us from our enemies.

As we crammed a cooler filled with drinks and snacks into Alex's already stuffed car, the final preparations for our trip across the country were complete. As I watched Jeff hug Alex at our front door, tears filled my eyes, but I quickly pushed them back. This was not a day to cry. This was a day to rejoice! Alex was driving for the first leg of our journey, and I was in the passenger seat. I took his hand and asked if he'd let me pray. I thanked God that we were where we were. I prayed for a safe trip, and I prayed for God to continue to be with Alex as he began this journey. After Alex and I both said, "Amen," he, obligingly, let me take a selfie of us before he put the car in reverse, and we drove down the road.

The trip took us a total of 33 hours of driving to get to Eureka. After the first day and close to 23 hours of driving, we finally stopped and stayed in a hotel room just outside of Salt Lake City, Utah. Along the way, we sang, talked, ate, slept, and watched the scenery of our gorgeous country go by.

With about six hours of our trip left to go, Alex and I stopped to use the restroom and fill the car up with gas. As the car eased into a parking space, we could see a homeless guy sitting on a curb, working on a beat-up bicycle, not far from where we parked. One of his tires had blown, and he was trying to figure out how to get it fixed. He was mumbling and cussing to himself as he wrestled with the bike. He was almost blocking the entrance to the restroom, and I could sense Alex becoming nervous and protective of me. A faint thought ran through the ticker of my brain to reach out to this man, but I hurried inside the bathroom instead.

Once I was back in the car, Alex left to go to the bathroom. As he exited the restroom, I watched as he stopped and talked to the man. I heard him tell the man "Stay here, man, I'll be right back."

As Alex got back into the car, he told me that the Holy Spirit was telling him to go buy this guy a new tire for his bike. I am not only awash with pride for Alex's desire to follow this direction, but also tired and (embarrassed to admit) a little frustrated at the extra time this will take. Our trip had taken us 27 hours of driving at this point. It was my son who set it straight in my head and reminded me whose we are. So, I quickly Googled the nearest Target, and before I knew it, we were standing in the bicycle tire section. Alex made a guess to the size of needed tire, then quickly grabbed snacks and drinks for the man as well.

"Bananas, the Holy Spirit is saying something to me about buying him bananas."

"Bananas?" I said.

"Yah, bananas. Something about his mother and bananas."

So we bought bananas.

When we returned to the gas station, the man now sat on the concrete, his broken bike beside him. Alex told me to stay in the car as he pulled out the tire and the snacks and walked toward the man. I'd like to say that something amazing happened in that moment, but the truth is Alex handed the guy the items, explained what he had brought to him, and then walked away. As we drove away, we were both wondering exactly how God was going to use this moment of obedience to draw this man in.

Chapter Forty-Two

My first impression of Eureka was that it was a dumpy, run-down town. The sky was gloomy, the buildings were outdated, and there were homeless people everywhere-walking down the streets, lying on the sidewalks, propped up against walls, everywhere. It is a good thing we had so much to do before I had to leave, otherwise I would have been engulfed in worry, but we had an apartment to prepare and furniture and groceries to purchase. We raced from store to store looking for the items we needed. We rented a U-Haul to bring a bed and mattress set we purchased at a local furniture store to Alex's new apartment. His 225 square foot studio wouldn't hold much, but we were able to find an organizing shelf that would hold a TV, and a couple of chairs that would collapse until needed that suited the tiny area. A very small table with foldable wings that fit perfectly in the leftover space was ordered and would soon be delivered. We purchased groceries and other essentials and stuffed every nook and cranny in and above the cupboards, the refrigerator/freezer, the only closet, under the bed, and in every crevice where something could be stored. It was important to me to have Alex settled into his new place before I left. It gave me a comfort and satisfied my need as his momma to make sure he was provided for, taken care of, and safe before I left in two days.

On Sunday, the school had a BBQ and orientation for students and families. It was an unusually warm day in Eureka, but it was a perfect day for us Illinoisans. The sun was out, and it was warm. As Alex and I drove onto the church and school campus, I was surprised by how small it was. The building itself was nothing that would catch your eye, but the property was flanked with enormous redwood trees, so tall you had to crane your neck out of the car window to see the tops, and so wide that you couldn't see around them. They stood like guardians tightly gathered, strong, experienced, and majestic. We had never seen anything like it. As I ran my hands down the trunk of one of the magnificent trees, I wondered how many students it had watched come to this place, how much healing had it witnessed, and how many times it had lifted praise to its maker?

The festivities were spread out on a large open area. There was food, tables, and tents set up. Alex and I watched people holding plates bulging with fresh BBQ and other amazing foods mingle with each other. For a second, I had a feeling of being in middle school at lunchtime with no one to sit with; however, we didn't walk but a few feet before people were welcoming us and helping us to feel included. We sat at a table with several other students, some with parents there and some without. They represented states like Minnesota, Wyoming, and Indiana.

On the far right of the field were tents. Alex had been telling me that they were going to be prophesying over people today, and he wanted to go. I have to admit, I was quite hesitant. When I was young, I went to a church where I saw a lot of hypocrisy, a lot of fake healing, and over reacting. I always felt like it was a show; very much like the Pharisees, making sure that everyone knew how special God thought you were. At this point in my life, I completely believe that God works in unexplainable spiritual ways. After all, I had seen and experienced miracles and the Holy Spirit's moving with my own eyes. It wasn't that I doubted that God gave some people the ability to prophesy, but I was leery that there was a whole tent of them. But this was Alex's day, and I wanted to participate in every single moment he wanted.

As we approached the tent, two people, a woman named Brittany and a man named Joel, asked Alex and me to sit down. We sat and made quick introductions to each other before the two began to pray. We four sat in silence as they waited to hear what the Lord had to say. It was Joel who began speaking to Alex first.

"Alex, I just keep hearing Him say this phrase, 'You will know the intricacies of who I am, and who I am in you.' And I think there's a lot that He wants to show you; that you're requisitioned right now because of your journey and your perspective to receive so much more. And He is just really proud of you, like how far you've come. Your commitment to God and yeah, He is just a really, really proud Father of who you are."

"Awesome. That's good," was Alex's response.

Brittany continued to pray, thanking Jesus for who He was. She then began to speak to me.

"I'm just trying to get a meaning behind the picture that I'm getting for you. But what I think the Lord is saying is that you have been really faithful during winter seasons."

She was silent again with her eyes closed. Then she opened her eyes and looked at me again.

"Sorry, I'm just listening for a second. Yeah, I just feel like He's really, really proud of you. Because it's easy, it's really easy to go after God in a good season. It's easy to be happy on your own and on your own strength and stir that up in yourself during those times. But when you really have to lean on the Lord and depend on him, when you have to lean on him during the hard seasons, and you do that and instead of running away, you run towards him, that's where we really build our faith, and where we really build on our walk with Christ. You know?"

I am overcome with tears immediately. How could this be anything but a word from God? This woman knows nothing about us except for our names.

"I feel like he's just saying, 'Well done.' He loves you, and he's proud of you. And I think it's those winter seasons that are going to take you further during the good times. I don't know if you're coming out of a difficult season or not, but I feel like this is a good time. I see the sun shining, and there's snow. And I see the sun shining and things are melting off. It's just good.

This is really, really good. He's proud of you. I hear Him saying, 'Joy comes in the morning', and His joy is here for you both. That this is a new day. This is a new season for your family."

She then began to pray, "Thank you for the endurance you have given them to walk through difficult times, to be faithful to you because you're so faithful to us, God. You're so faithful to us, and so constant, Lord. It's a testing for us to be faithful back, but thank you Jesus for your peace; the peace that surpasses understanding. Thank you, Lord. But a new day is dawning, a new day, a new season. Lord, I just ask that you show them your goodness in ways that they haven't seen before. Lord, I ask you to show them where you're shinning your light; speak newness over them."

She then began to talk to Alex.

"I have to say I see pink roses now. Lord, I thank you for your pink roses: hope, your sweetness, God. Alex, you are getting equipped this year. That may sound generic, because I think everybody in your class is getting equipped this year, but specifically for you. I feel like you are going to really grab hold of the tools that you get and actually apply them to your life. Because we can get so many tools, and we can be given a lot and know what the right thing to do is, and want someone else to do it for us, instead of us doing it ourselves. I really feel like you are going to be equipped and carry that stuff and actually walk all that stuff out. Instead of just knowing it, you're going to do it. You are going to be an example to other people because of that. People are going to see and say, 'I know what he could have done in that situation, but he didn't.' People are going to see you do the right thing. You may be a first-year student, but you are going to be such an example. You are a leader, and an example to other people, and I want to encourage you in that. As you get it, you will be empowered. When it's hard to do what you know you are being led to do; just trust that."

"Good word. Good word," Alex replied. Then Joel began speaking to Alex again.

"He trusts you; you're a good steward of the important things of God. You're honorable. You're a really honorable person."

Brittany breaks in again, "I also see purity over you. Which can mean many different things, but it is the goodness of God, and it is who God is. He is so pure, you know? It's not just purity in the sense that we always think of; it's the purity in your heart, your motives, and in everything you do. You know people can manipulate love, but I just see a purity over you."

As Alex thanks them for their time, I am almost speechless. He and I step outside of the tent. Alex steals a glance at me and sees the tears streaming down my face. He smiles and laughs a little and throws an arm around my shoulders and pulls me to his side as we walk away.

Later that night, when we get back to Alex's apartment, I make a video of every single space, so I can have something to use to envision where he is while I am all the way back in Illinois. We blow up an air mattress for me to sleep on, and it barely fits in his teeny tiny place. Once the mattress is filled to its capacity with air, there is barely room to slip between the mattress and through the bathroom door.

Alex and I talk about life, dreams, and challenges deep into the night. My heart is so full. I reach across the small space between us and offer my hand to him. He takes it, and we hold hands silently for a moment as all the pain, hurt, and fear of the last seven years passes between us, as we both drift off to sleep.

Chapter Forty-Three

My alarm wakes me with a start at 4 a.m. I quickly turn it off, so as not to wake Alex, and stumble into the bathroom to get ready for my 6 a.m. flight home. I can feel a heaviness in my heart threatening to overtake me, but it is a different heaviness than I have felt so many times over the last seven years. This time it is not one of fear. This time it is not one of hopelessness. This time it is just the sadness of physically leaving my son in a strange place thousands of miles from home. Realizing I only have a few more moments left with Alex for some time to come, I will myself not to cry. I quickly get dressed and then begin making his favorite scrambled eggs for breakfast.

We are soon heading to the airport. As I reach across the car and place my hand on his leg, he reaches down and grabs it. I remember a time when my hand would envelope his, but now it is clearly the other way around. I tell him how proud of him I am, how I knew he would get to this place in life, and how much gratitude I have for how God has walked with us every step of the way.

When we pull up to the airport, I have tears in my eyes, but I am desperately trying not to let this be the last thing Alex sees. After he pulls my luggage from the trunk of his car, he turns to me. I smile and look him directly in the eyes.

"I am going to miss you so much, but I know you are going to do great things here."

With tears in his eyes, he wrapped his arms around me, and tears slip down my face.

"Thank you for everything; for loving me, for believing in me, and for fighting for me. I love you."

"I love you more than you will ever know. Take care of yourself," I say as I begin to walk away. Then I turn to watch Alex get into his car and wave as he pulls away.

I walk to the counter to check into my flight. I'm running late, so I don't have time to fall apart. I make it through TSA and quickly board the small plane. When I am finally settled in my assigned seat, I can no longer hold back the tears. And as the plane begins its takeoff, I am sobbing tears of thankfulness, as the truth of this moment finally hits me. By the grace of God, we really were all going to be O.K.

Afterword

May 2020

In just a few weeks Alex is graduating from his final year at BSSD. If not for the Coronavirus Pandemic of 2020, Jeff and I would be there to witness the ceremony, but sadly no live ceremony will be held. The past three years have been an amazing journey of physical, mental, and spiritual growth and healing for Alex. I have been in awe as I have witnessed it all. Next fall, he will begin working as a member of the staff at Surge School of Transformation, a new ministry school in Atlanta, Georgia. He continues to seek and follow The Holy Spirit at every turn.

January 2021

God continues to amaze! For years as I battled for Alex's life, I heard the Holy Spirit whisper, "He's going to work with kids. He's going to be a youth pastor. You just wait and see how I use this boy!"

And true to that promise, Alex was asked to become the first youth pastor for Resurgence ATL, an Atlanta area church plant that launched Oct. 7, 2017. Alex has been given the opportunity to establish and create a youth group program for kids 6th-12th grade. There were 20 kids who came to the first youth group meeting on January 31. He also continues his volunteer ministry position at Surge School of Transformation.

Praise the Lord.
Praise God in his sanctuary;
 praise him in his mighty heavens.
Praise him for his acts of power;
praise him for his surpassing greatness.
Praise him with the sounding of the
trumpet,
praise him with the harp and
Lyre.
Praise him with tambourine and dancing,
praise him with the strings and flute,
praise him with resounding cymbals.
Let everything that has breath
Praise the Lord.

–Psalm 150

Epilogue

The following are writings from Alex while at BSSD.

December 2017

Yah know, when I came here I knew how to breathe
really well.
Well... at least I thought I did.

I entered into this season more hurting and broken than
I'd care to admit.
Actually, I think I was drowning inside of my own
sentiments.
A victim to a lifetime of hiding behind mask after mask
had taken its toll.
I came here with a knowing that I had to roll:
Roll away the stones of pain from the crevices of my
battered and war-torn heart.
Roll away the slowly fading memories of a life of
rejection, delusion, and betrayal.

The moment I crossed the Humboldt County line, it was
as if an early morning fog rolled into my mind.
The blindness of it enough to drive me insane.
Drowning in an ocean of the unknown
The weight of not knowing where I'm going.

Have I finally gotten myself into a hole too deep to be pulled from?

I know God saved me from hell, but can He save me from this self-dug well?

I still cannot stand the thought that I've hindered my own growth.
That at the end of my life I'll stand before the Almighty as He speaks of things that SHOULD have been....
Instead of things that are.

I can't dwell on the thoughts that I've wasted too much time.
They. Are. Not. Mine.
I am not the compilation of my ghosts and failures.

My value is not weighted against the bones of my past.
"I Am that I Am," says my God, "and You are who I say You are."
He calls me His Son. His Beloved and Redeemed. His Chosen.
His Trusted One. His Armor Bearer.
Unrelenting are the intoxicating love letters from Heaven to My Heart.

And what's more is that I AM WORTHY of them,
To receive these things because my Daddy tells me so.

I will no longer get caught up in what I can't see.
So focused on my toes that I can't perceive the end of my own nose!

I will no longer be bound up by the lies that I'm blinded by my own surmise.
That I can't hear how much He bestows upon me.
Masquerading the arrogance of my ignorance.

You see; this walk is so much easier than I've made it.

He's laid it all out for me to find.
Hidden and concealed behind the humanity of my flesh.
So that this King can seek out and find while in His rest.

Once, I allowed the morality of my humanity to outweigh the value of what I could see inside of me....

How could I ever love you when I thought nothing but less of myself?

It's lies.

My God breathes truth,
Truth that is not skewed by the lens of self-hatred and indulgences.

A new sun peeks over the mountains of my failure.
It's cold where I sit. A dense, consuming fog envelopes
me.
I desperately plea with my heart to move on, but I am
paralyzed by the skeletons I can feel re-converging upon
my cries.

A stream of light suddenly cuts through the fog of my
past.
As the light grazes my cheek it whispers to my heart
"there is so much gold here.
Let go of the past and let Me have it."
What I've learned this semester,
Is that I. Am. Worthy.
I'm worthy.
I am worthy to be loved and accepted by you.
I am worthy to receive His love.
I am worthy to walk away from a life of self-
condemnation and bitterness.
I am worthy to allow me to love myself.

And there it is.
As if typing this out unplugged from my mind, my
fingers have co-labored with my soul to prophesy to the
consciousness that stands before you today.
This perspective shift has erected a directive inside of
me that can NOT be stolen.
My God has met me in the cesspools of my mess,
And He HAS NOT loved me any less.

It does not matter the dirt or the shame or vain I feel.
It does not matter the bane of my brain clatter.
A veil has been lifted up from my veins.
It cannot return or remain.
"IT IS FINISHED," is written inside my name.

June 2018

It's in the early morning hours I feel the most alive.
I don't have to contrive ability, creativity, or identity.
It's just a part of me.

It's like the early morning air is calling me into more.
I can feel a hand guiding me out from the safety of my
shores.
My heart is longing for more.
Yet I cannot stand to be here.

Self-sabotage creeps up through my veins to steal joy
from this moment,
And, suddenly I'm no longer able to contain the visions
of my future.
But I won't let that dictate the healing of my sutures.

I find rest in the dew on early mornings.
Peace greets me, gently pressing at my chest.
Reminding me I don't sit in that mess.

I don't have to strive.
I don't have to hide.
I don't have to ride out the storm.
I just get to be.

It's like in those moments I feel the greatness I was
created for.

In those hours that greatness doesn't feel far off,
Déjà vu of the ventures coming.

I hear the groans of my city on these mornings of self-
exploration.
The atmosphere of prophetic visions over my life billows
onto the city.
Heaven's perspective begins to erect my directive.

I feel the air begin to churn.
Vibrating, folding, and molding into the breath of God.
This place is boiling.
I can feel the electricity of expectancy.
This city is about to explode with promise,
With excellence,
With hope.

The depression that's hung over this city like a fog is
being enraptured in Heaven's smog.

Get ready for the unlocking.
I see a door.
It's unlocked and cracked.

It's an invitation to influence,
A Correlation between the richness of this world and the
next.
I see doors swinging wide for us.
Get ready to step into Heaven's unrest for our city.

This beauty between cannot be unseen, and it's time to redeem the crime grafted into our Vine for such a time, as this.

Can you feel it groaning?
Do you feel the Earth, growling beneath your feet.
It's shaking.
Longing for you and I to be revealed so that we can devise with the Almighty to rise and delete the foes over our seats for this city.

I hear Him saying,
"Get ready, my child,
You're about to ride,
Out from these ashes,
From behind these lies,
For Heaven's arrived,
To sum up our tries,
Truth is splitting in,
To cover all of this sin."

Our city will follow in our wake
They're hurting and burning in their hearts,
They're yearning for more,
Will we invite them to what's in store?

Will we allow our bout with unrighteousness to be put down for the
sake of the world?
We're not chained to the thoughts that we're still broken,

But to the truth that we're whole
That we carry things that feed the needs of our city.

Take a stand with me to plead for this place.
But it's not really so much a plea as it is stance in our
inheritance.
Dream on, Dreamer.
For those dreams dreamt on starry nights bring the
breakthrough that sends the Heavens a-flight.

CLOSENESS

"What if it's all for you right now? What if this season isn't for what you can pass along? What if the outpouring is a byproduct of the infilling? Is it enough if it's all just for you? I will never let your position succeed our secret place."

Intimacy sees into me, but what if I do not see into myself?
Search me? Well then, tell me what you find.
The caverns of my heart seem so empty. Roll away the façade of self-love.
I will not settle for counterfeits,
Only You.
More of You.
As my heart grows prostrate, I reach out my hands.
I lay them on feet.
Glowing bronze feet.
They do not hurt me; they are warm and inviting.
Gentle, healing, and soothing.
I see those nails gliding painlessly into my hands and through His predestined holes.

August 2019

I have realized that it is not the enemy's cunningness, nor my inability to remain pure, that has brought me here. I am standing between two worlds: a life sold-out, and a life yet to be sold. Transition begets great faith. I am here, at this place, because of the kindness and goodness of my Father, a Father who will not send His Son into battle naked, untaught, and ignorant; a Father who is strong and faithful through my cries of pain, and pleas through the torment. Calvary cries of victories unbeknownst to me. The tears are healing. They melt this hard, hurt heart. So, all the more, I must be still. I must feel. I must rest.

Alex and Mike Weaver of Big Daddy Weave

Alex and I in Eureka, CA.

From left: Alex, Monique, Jeff, & Drew

Connect with the Author on Facebook @

Monique Davis-Author's page

Some names in this story
were changed.

61152491R00166